CHRISTIAN SEX ETHICS

An Introduction

CHRISTIAN SEX ETHICS

An Introduction

By
V. A. DEMANT

HARPER & ROW, PUBLISHERS
New York and Evanston

FIRST EDITION

LIBRARY OF CONGRESS CATALOG CARD NUMBER: 64–15481

CONTENTS

1   Masculine and Feminine   *page*   9

2   Chastity in Christendom   26

3   Eros and Romantic Love   43

4   The Marriage Covenant   59

5   Living Together   73

6   Sex and Civilisation   90

7   The Erotic Obsession of the Twentieth Century   107

PREFACE

A UNIVERSITY teacher who is also sometimes a preacher has the advantage, which may be painful, of being available for questioning, advice and perhaps contradiction by his teaching colleagues and by the pupil generation. This makes him subject to surprises. When he delivers a piece of knowledge which he thinks is valuable or offers a message which he believes his hearers are in want of, he may frequently be chilled to find that no one is impressed. Contrariwise, something ground out because an utterance is required, without the lift of feeling helpful, often elicits a response that it has spoken to someone's condition. Both these situations are salutary, the first humiliating, the second humbling.

When it was suggested to me that in addition to my regular instruction on Christian Ethics I should expound the Church's teaching on sex, love and marriage, there was no doubt about the need. The lectures here printed represent my attempt to meet it. They were originally delivered before a university audience composed mostly of undergraduates of both sexes. In this case I was fortunate in discovering that they were welcomed to the extent of inducing requests for publication.

A university audience has at least to put up a show of requiring documentary support for verbal pronouncements. I have therefore mentioned the literature I have used and recommend. Where it is not quoted in the body of the lectures, references to it will be found at the end of the book.

V.A.D.

Christ Church,
Oxford

1

MASCULINE AND FEMININE

I AM offering these lectures on Christian Sex Ethics for the following reasons. The teaching of the Church about right and wrong in sexual behaviour is publicly referred to in two ways. One, by those who are alarmed at the looseness and licence in sexual relations today, and who have some idea that it is due to loss of Christian moral standards in general, or to mere remnants of those standards unsupported by full Christian faith. This alarm is not confined to convinced Christians; many secular humanists, for social and moral reasons, are worried by an increase in sexual promiscuity; experimentation by the young; the casual breaking of the marriage tie, often repeated by the same persons; by crimes of violence with sexual motives; by fornication being taken for granted as harmless and ceasing to be shocking; and in consequence by the appearance of abnormal sex cravings in such things as the Lolita situation and the sex kitten image; not to speak of sexual assaults on the old and of an alleged growth in homosexuality.

Concern about all this is naturally bound up with the knowledge that Christianity has been the prevailing religion in our culture, and it is therefore inferred that the sexual deterioration has some connection with the weakening of the hold which Christian belief has upon the population as a whole. This is not wholly misjudged, but it is a pity that one result of this alarm is the widespread false impression that for Christianity sexual misdemeanour is the only immorality, and that breach of the Christian sexual code is the only or the worst sin.

But, now, in the second place, there is a vast body of modern opinion which holds that the Christian standard in sexual relations has been too rigorous and restrictive; that it is unnatural and impossible to observe for men and women in general. It is widely believed that the Christian religion denigrates sex or regards it as a menace to the fullest and best kinds of life. Thomas Hardy in *Jude the Obscure* put it thus: "a religion in which sexual love is regarded as at its best a frailty, and at its worst damnation." Influenced by some psychological teaching, many writers today contend that the strict moral sexual code of Christianity has introduced complexes and disturbances in the human psyche, and turned a perfectly natural force into the seat of a perpetual bad conscience. Gibbon and Lecky were inclined to this view. They have their followers in R. Briffault, author of *The Mothers*, and in Bertrand Russell who wrote: "the Christian view of marriage and sex is an irrational system of taboo created by mediaeval superstition and oriental asceticism. The fact that it is embedded in Christian ethics has made Christianity, throughout its whole history, a tendency towards mental disorders and unwholesome views of life."[1]

I will deal with some of the issues raised by these criticisms in later lectures. Now I am only concerned to point out that both defenders and opponents of the Christian Faith have to bring into the centre of the picture the main Christian tradition on sexual relations as a colossal influence, whether they regard it as good or bad. Therefore it is well that there should be from time to time some information on what that tradition contains. That is what I aim to present in outline, with some interpretation as a defender of it.

Whether in the end you are convinced that the Christian teaching on sex ethics, with its two main tenets of continence outside marriage and fidelity within marriage, is worth living by, involving as it does a real discipline, or whether you conclude that this is far beyond your powers, at least you will know where you are.

Anyway, many are growing up and living in a world of conflicting standards of judgment and are confronted with a great deal of sexual stimulation, often camouflaged in the press and cheap publications as information or as warning or as mere news. Yet they are in frightful ignorance of what it is all about, namely the love relationship of men and women, and completely in the dark as to what the Christian sex ethics are.

Moreover, the young and also the not so young are offered a torrent of alleged guidance on the marriage problem, on sex education, on genital fulfilment and the rest, as if you could sort it all out for yourselves. A friend of mine once shared a railway compartment with a young American couple, where in the intervals between mutual signs and acts of endearment, the young man consulted the open pages of Kinsey's work *The Sexual Behaviour of the Human Male*. One wonders sometimes how the human race has avoided complete insanity if it is supposed to have lived in ignorance of all the pitfalls this mass of literature sets out to enlighten us about.

I should remind you that Christianity has not produced what is called 'the sex problem'. That problem is inherent in human existence, as the literature of the world makes quite clear. This is because in the human being sex is never a purely instinctive urge. Homo, neither eats nor makes love as a mere biological creature. (I use the Latin *homo* for the human being, man or woman.) The powerful biological urge in mankind is interwoven with at least three other layers of human existence. There is, secondly, the psychic or emotional attachment between a man and a woman, epitomised in the experience of 'falling in love' and being in love. This we will call *eros* or erotic love, and it runs in many directions outside the venereal act of sexual intercourse. The venereal aspect we will call venus, or just coitus. Thirdly the venereal experience is closely geared to the social act of living together in most cases where *eros* leads to it, both in marriage and in extra-marital unions. Such unions are often the most tyrannical of bonds because they depend entirely upon the partners keeping emotionally all the time up to scratch. Fourthly, these three levels of erotic experience have to be adjusted to the fact that the man and the woman have individual goals and interests, and the strain between these and the love relationship is the seat of much conflict in and between the partners.

Now, this complex of forces in human sexuality makes its own difficulties quite apart from the imposition of religious moral standards. Mankind has always had to find some way of dealing with it, and the religious traditions of the race have been directly concerned with its practical solution. Mere talk and information and research will not help by themselves.

I believe that the sex problem today, in the sense of venereal experience, is isolated far too much from the other aspects of the love relationship in men and women. Therefore I have planned these lectures in order to place it in its wider setting, and in order to show that Christian Sex Ethics have a much more positive context than that of prohibitions, or of restriction in sexual opportunity within certain well prescribed limits.

We start therefore with the polarity of masculine and feminine, or gender, as attended to in religion. It has been attended to because mankind, at a certain stage of consciousness, has been impressed by the problem that the division of *homo* into male and female is both an essential fact of human existence, and at the same time has given the human race one of its most troublesome tasks.

By gender, I mean that mysterious relation of powers, of which sexuality is the concrete human expression. The relation has often been described as one of polarity, like the positive and negative in electricity (positive and negative being conventional terms without any suggestion of relative value, or like the north and south poles of the earth's structure. The idea is that where there is one there must be the other, like the two ends of a stick, which are on the same plane and yet are in a sense opposites. But where the poles are forces and not just positions, there is a tension which seems due to the fact that they can never be completely separated or completely fused in one.[2]

Now, when confronting any important part of human existence the Christian theologian asks certain questions. Does it belong to the order of creation, like matter and spirit, the family and race? Or does it belong to the order of history like the state, nationality, civilisation and science, things that are not found among men everywhere but arise under certain historical conditions? And also, does it belong to the fallen nature of man, either as the working out of a sinful principle like aggression, or as a device to curb the effects of egoism, like the coercive aspects of law and order?

We can answer quite easily that gender belongs not to the order of history but to the order of creation, for it runs all through humanity and beyond. The other question is not so easy; does gender exist because of some kind of fall from true existence? Such a view has some able defenders who are so impressed with the enmities and problems of sexuality among humans, that they think man's spiritual nature can only be tied up with biological urges by some original calamity.

They hold that the only true human being is *androgyne*, namely man-woman, or rather a whole of which male and female are subsequent dissociations. Plato in *The Symposium* puts this view into the mouth of Aristophanes who pictures *homo* as originally globular in shape. These first humans tried to carry heaven by assault and were punished for their pride by being sliced in two. The two halves are always trying to unite; hence eros is the pursuit of wholeness, an effort to overcome disunion. This, however, is not Plato's own view. The idea of original *homo* as androgyne has been expounded in this century at some length by Nicholas Berdyaev in several of his works.[3] He brings to his support Jacob Boehme, in the seventeenth century, and other mystics, as well as ancient writings like the Zohar of the Jewish Kabbala, and many gnostic documents—all of which suggest that sexuality is in some way a fall from the original Adam state which is androgynous. Although such speculations influenced some early Christian writers, they are foreign to the central Biblical and church tradition and derive mostly from movements of pre-Christian origin in the Hellenistic world, especially that of gnostic speculation. The main Christian stream of thought is closely geared to the Bible which insists that male and female are part of the creation as God wills it to be, and on which He looked and saw that it was good. He is maker of Earth as well as of Heaven.

Having concluded that gender, or sexuality, is of the order of creation, we have to ask: how deep does it go? Does it run into the Godhead itself? First of all, we observe that it does not run all through the created world. The stars have no gender, though they have male and female names; inanimate nature has no

15

gender, though perhaps discoveries of negative and positive protons, on top of the more familiar negative and positive electrons, may be interpreted as a kind of polarity in matter, similar to gender. Anyhow, in its obvious form gender is confined to the biological world. But it does not spread all over that. There are lowly forms of life which multiply by division, and others which unite without propagation. The world of the amoeba and such like, is full of virgin births.

Gender, then, does not mark the whole created work of God. But, it certainly marks the human creation, and as man is in Christian theology the most significant part of creation, made in a unique sense in the image of God, it is legitimate to ask whether there is something in the divine origin corresponding to gender in the human image, and of course whether the image in man has gender or is above or behind this kind of polarity.

We must not be misled into thinking that God as revealing Himself in the Bible has gender because His name and titles are masculine. Elohim is an abstract plural; the consonantal name YHVH, corrupted to our Jehovah, is probably an extension of the word *Hu*, meaning he, as God is called by other Arab tribes at times of religious revival—the One, the Unnameable, without suggestion of gender.[4] It has the force of a providential presence. And where the Lord is thought of as father, as in Moses' words to Pharaoh: "Israel is my first-born son," or in Hosea and Jeremiah's analogy of human fatherliness for God's divine love for Israel, the emphasis is not on fatherhood in contrast to motherhood, or on fatherhood as generative, but rather on the moral authority and lordship of history which later acquired benevolent attributes of loving care.

Nevertheless, in spite of the complete absence of the idea of God generating the world (which is His creation and not His offspring) and in spite of 'fatherhood' having authoritative and providential rather than male meanings, there have been from time to time voices in Christian thought and devotion declaring that this imagery gave a masculine one-sidedness to the idea of God. One of the best known statements of this theme was made by the Dame Julian of Norwich in her *Revelations of Divine Love.* This fourteenth-century English mystical writer, with considerable philosophical powers, subordinates theological precision to the requirements of her devotional insight. As we listen to a few passages we must remember that she is using this gender imagery to convey the relation of God to man—and not formulating a gender theory of persons in the Trinity. Here is one: "And furthermore I saw that the Second Person, which is our Mother as anent the substance, that dearworthy Person is become our Mother as anent the Sense-soul. For we are double by God's making; that is to say Substantial and Sensual. Our substance is the higher part, which we have in our Father, God Almighty; and the Second Person of the Trinity is our Mother in Nature, in making of our Substance: in whom we are grounded and rooted. And He is our Mother in Mercy, in taking our sense part."

What are we to make of this language? Dame

Julian is a sufficiently good theologian to realise that the second Person of the Trinity—the Word of God, the Logos, the Son—who took flesh in the man Jesus Christ, is the agent of creation as well as the Saviour. Julian is not really attempting to make the Son feminine in relation to Father and Holy Spirit, for she uses this gender symbolism in a quite different way in a passage like this: "I understood that the High Might of the Trinity is our Father, and the deep Wisdom of the Trinity is our Mother, and the great love of the Trinity is our Lord; and all this we have in Nature and in the making of our Substance."[5] But we can see why this language is used for the relation of God and man; it is because the tender, healing and forgiving action of God seems especially a feminine characteristic. Further, it is in the Son that redemptive suffering takes place, and the Son is the one person of the Trinity to take human flesh.

Let us now turn from these speculations about the nature of God to His creative work. We have noticed that gender covers part of the created world but not all of it; it covers all but the most rudimentary forms of life. Gender covers all human existence, and there it is much more than a biological fact, though it is rooted in the life stream. Gender colours man's psyche or soul and gender symbolism, even sex symbolism, is used to express religious relationships involving God, man, the Church, the soul.

One question which arises is whether the Priestly document of Genesis (i. 27), by joining together the statements "God created man in His own image" and "male and female created he them," conveys an inspired insight that the image does not belong to each gender separately but to the two together. Those who have thought that neither man nor woman is complete *homo*, but that only the androgyne is perfectly human, give this interpretation to the text. I do not think it can carry that weight. Karl Barth in his Church Dogmatics does consider "male and female created he them" as a statement about the image. Neither man nor woman alone has the divine image.[6] This view has met with serious criticism. But anyhow, the coupling of the creation of man in the divine image with the male and female differentiation, does suggest at least that they are complementary parts of human existence by the will of the Creator.

To turn now to the Fall story. It denies straightaway that the fact of gender and sex is the result of the Fall. Then, note that the thing taken is not anything wrong, evil or morally bad. It is the fruit of a tree, "good to look at and to eat". Not even an apple is mentioned. G. K. Chesterton said: "The apple that Eve ate was an orange and the peel has been lying about ever since." It was the fruit of the tree of knowledge of good and evil—and for ancients this meant not so much moral good and evil, as pleasure and pain, joy and misery, fortune and ill fortune. The widespread identification of apple with the forbidden fruit is probably due to the Greek and Latin words for apple being also used for fruit in general. Martin Buber is, I think, right in rejecting the idea that sexual desire is the forbidden fruit. He says that such an idea "is precluded by the fact of the creation of man and woman as sexually mature beings and by the concept of 'becoming like God' which is coupled with the 'knowledge of good and evil': this God is supra-sexual". Buber then expounds his own interpretation: "Knowledge of good and evil means nothing else than: cognisance of the two opposites which the early literature of mankind designated by these two terms; fortune and misfortune, order and chaos, light and darkness etc." God knows these oppositions but He is above them; He knows them intellectually but He does not experience them. A superior familiar encompassing of opposites is denied to man who, despite his 'likeness' to God, has a part only in that which is created and not in creation. He knows oppositeness only by his situation within it.[7] And one of the forms of this oppositeness is that of masculine and feminine — 'they knew they were naked'. We might say that one consequence of the Fall is to turn complementary different things — polar opposites — into rivalries and contradictions.

We must now glance at some expressions of gender symbolism in the language of the Church. The first that comes to mind perhaps is the figure of husband and wife as symbols of the relation of Christ and His Church. This has the authority of the Epistle to the Ephesians[8], but it runs through a great deal of the liturgical and informal piety as well as the thought of Christian devotion. Our Lord is the authority for this metaphor of Christ and His Church. Christ likens Himself to the bridegroom (Mark ii. 18-20; cf. John iii. 29); the Kingdom is likened to a marriage feast

(Matt. xxii. 2-12; xxv. 1-13; Luke xii. 35 ff.). In Revelation the Church is the Bride (xix. 7 ff.; xxi. 2, 9; xxii. 17). One of the most interesting much later commentaries on this theme is to be found in the work of a seventeenth-century Christian Platonist, Ralph Cudworth. In a writing called *The Union of Christ and the Church; in a Shadow*,[9] Cudworth asserts that the union of man and woman is not a mere metaphor or symbol, but is a divinely appointed copy or image of Christ's unity with the Church. Husband and wife are the type of which Christ and the Church are the archetype.

The incarnation is often likened to the marriage union. Origen wrote: "For to this (union of the Word with human nature) more than to anything else can the passage of Scripture be applied, they shall both be one flesh, and they are no longer two but one flesh. For the Word of God is to be thought of as being more 'in one flesh' with his soul than a man is with his wife."[10]

There had been attempts among some early Christian speculators to liken the relation of persons in the Trinity to partners in marriage. Augustine discusses them in his treatise, *De Trinitate*.[11] He says it is a faulty analogy but makes some interesting contributions of his own. Augustine writes that the text in Genesis dealing with the image "says that human nature itself, which is complete only in both sexes, was made in the image of God, and it does not separate the woman from the image of God which it signifies". But marriage is no analogue to the eternal generation of the Son, nor to the eternal procession of the Holy

Spirit. Only in the most general way could the one flesh of two persons in marriage be a metaphor for the relation of the persons in the divine unity.

To complete the account of gender symbolism, we must look at one more set of ideas. The most frequent is the idea that in some way the human creature is feminine to God. This sometimes, in the mystics, takes the form of seeing God or Christ as the spouse of the soul. In the case of women mystics like St. Teresa and Angela of Foligno, the distinctly erotic language has shocked people who misunderstood the symbolism; or it has been used to support the theory that all desire for mystical union is due to thwarted sex life. But the answer to this has been well given by Mlle Simone de Beauvoir who is not over-sympathetic to Christianity. Of St. Teresa, who had great physical and organic crises in her mystical states, Mlle de Beauvoir writes: "It would be false to interpret her emotions as a simple 'sublimation' of sex; there is not first an unavowed desire that later takes the form of divine love. The amoureuse herself is not at first the prey of a desire without object which is later to become fixed on an individual man; it is the presence of the lover that arouses in her a desire directly orientated to him. Similarly, St. Teresa in a single process seeks to be united with God, and lives out this union in her body; she is not the slave of her nerves and her hormones; one must admire rather the intensity of her flesh . . . She poses in a most intellectual fashion the dramatic problem of the relation between the individual and the transcendent Being; she lived out, as a woman, an experience whose meaning goes far beyond the fact of her sex."[12]

Then there is St. John of the Cross whose long treatises on contemplative prayer are commentaries on his poems. If one did not know who wrote the poems one could suppose that many of them described the ecstasy of a young girl keeping secret tryst with her lover. Take this from his best known song of the soul, *Upon a Gloomy Night*:

> "Within my flowering breast
> Which only for himself entire I save
> He sank into his rest
> And all my gifts I gave
> Lulled by the airs with which the cedars wave."[13]

Another version of this love imagery is to be found in the beautiful work of Ramon Lull called *The Book of the Lover and the Beloved* where the gender symbolism is reversed, God being called the Beloved, and the soul is the Lover.[14]

I will now take as an outstanding example of this symbolism of the soul and God, under the image of the beloved and the lover, the sermons of St. Bernard on the *Song of Songs*. He there takes the love of the bride for her bridegroom as the human type of the soul's pure love of God. Here are a few sentences. By conversion the soul is reformed and rendered conformable to the word in love.

> "Such conformity marries the soul to the Word, when she shows herself like by will to Him to

whom she is like by nature, loving as she is loved
. . . A great thing is love, but there are degrees in
it. The bride stands in the highest. For sons love,
but think of their inheritance, and, while they
fear in some way to lose this, they reverence more
but love less, Him from whom the heritage is
expected. I hold in suspicion the love which the
hope of acquiring something seems to support. It
is weak, if perchance, should the hope be with-
drawn, it is either quenched or diminished. It is
impure if it desires ought else. Pure love is not
mercenary. Pure love gathers no strength from
hope, nor suffers loss through distrust. This love
the bride hath, because it is all that the bride is . . .
In this the bride abounds, with this the bridegroom
is content. He seeks nought else; nor hath she
ought else."[15]

We have now looked at four ways in which the love
of man and woman has been thought of as a symbol of
theological mysteries: of the bond of Christ and the
Church: of the divine and human natures in Christ: of
the Persons in the Trinity; of the soul's unity with God.
If these are not all equally inspired insights they tell in
the direction of supposing the gender relation to be one
of a number of polarities which are not themselves of
the order of gender but which can be likened to the
polarity of male and female.

Also, earlier in this lecture, we observed a deep-
rooted sense that the masculine-feminine polarity runs
very deep in the universe, so that many religions and

philosophies have sought in it almost the key to existence. However exaggerated this insight may be, it does testify to the fact that sex is an aspect of man's being and must be understood as representing much more than the instinctive and emotional desire of a man and woman for possession of each other. Sexuality does not necessarily and always issue in the search for venereal union. Venereal experience is therefore often renounced in the cause of more specialised expressions of man's personal vocation.

All this surely is enough to make us suspect that there is some mistake in the idea that gender and sexual love are undervalued or depreciated in the thought of Christianity. In the next lecture we shall see how the Church on the contrary has recognised their enormous power, creative and destructive, and has therefore set limits to their unbounded expression.

2

CHASTITY IN CHRISTENDOM

AFTER the picture of the religious significance of gender and sexual love which I gave in my first lecture, it seems a narrowing of the vision to speak of chastity, for chastity means binding the sexual relation of men and women within certain well defined limits, and in some respects its complete renunciation. That sounds rather negative, but it is only limiting in the same way as are the banks put up to canalise a wide and shallow river, converting it into a deeper and more powerful stream of water in order to work a mill. Chastity narrows in order to deepen the erotic power in mankind, and in order to let it minister to the full development of human life which is much more than the field of erotic forces.

Chastity in Christendom has a twofold *rationale*. In the first place, there is some resemblance between religious and sexual experience. Both take the individual beyond the boundaries of himself and his social relationships; both open him to realities unattainable by the rational intellect; both introduce him to powers greater than his own, to God in his religion, to the life-stream in his sex. For all that the divine and eternal realm surpasses in depth and width the scope of erotic experience, both in unequal degrees meet the psychic need of human beings for roots in a world which transcends the self. That is why in many faiths religious and sexual rituals are closely geared to one another. It is also the reason why sex, when obsessive, becomes a rival to religious faith. The reverse is also true: in periods of irreligion fulfilment of some of the needs which religious resources would otherwise meet is sought for through maniacal intensification of sexual demands.

In the second place, gender and sexuality immerse mankind in the cosmic process and are therefore sensed as menacing to the person and his freedom. The sex impulse is fundamentally impersonal in its nature and racial in its goal. It keeps mankind within the sphere of necessity. It does not by itself minister to the creative power of the individual or of society. In fact the religions and the literatures have often expressed the sentiment that sex is a premonition of death. Only when sexuality is imbued with a personal element from outside itself does it subserve the development of the whole human being. Sexuality becomes imbued with this personal element by the social and moral sexual codes of mankind; at a higher degree by the unique appearance of personal love in the West; and conclusively by making a skilled work of art out of fidelity in married love.

Put negatively chastity in the Christian tradition confines the act of venus or sexual intercourse to marriage; and as we shall see in the next lecture, it is Christianity which has mainly helped to set this marital venereal experience in the wider context of eros—

being in love. Being in love, however—in the romantic sense of the word—is not the only or even the necessary condition of fruitful and happy marriage. There is a second limit set by Christian chastity: there is to be sexual fidelity to the other partner in marriage until that marriage is terminated under God by the death of the partner. These two limits rule out therefore adultery, that is to say fornication when one or both parties are married; they rule out fornication between the unmarried, pre-marital venereal union, free-love, and trial marriages. They rule out also homosexual practices and other counterfeits of the normal heterosexual act of intercourse. This is not to say that all deviations from the standards of chastity are regarded as equally sinful. Christian moral theology has graded such deviations in various ways in order to indicate their relative seriousness.

Now let us look at the matter positively. These limits or prohibitions are the underside of a teaching about the fulfilment of sexual love—which Christianity maintains is only reached within those limits. Chastity, in this sense of experiencing venereal sexual union only within the marriage covenant, abstinence outside it, and in some cases continual virginity, has been enjoined and commended in the Bible and the Church without much explanation. Explanation seems required today, roughly since the nineteenth century when adultery became the theme of the modern novel. And especially in the last forty years when it began to be said that sex was in a mess because it had been hushed up. Mr. C. S. Lewis wrote twenty years ago—"but for the past twenty years it has not been hushed up—it has been chatted about all day long. Yet it is still in a mess. If hushing up had been the cause of the trouble, ventilation would have set it right. But it has not."[1]

This is to say, for a century sex has become a problem in a new sense. It has always set a practical problem because the allurement of 'the exquisite pleasure', as the Greeks called it, was of such power that it conflicted with other human demands, and because the mighty force of love brings suffering as well as joy, destruction as well as creation, discord as well as harmony, hatred as well as tenderness.

Now today sex is more of an intellectual problem, raising such question as: what is the place of sex in life?—and have the age-long codes of sexual behaviour been misguided? Can't men and women be natural and spontaneous in their love life? So, very much as D. H. Lawrence said, we have got sex in the head instead of where it ought to be, in the blood. Until the last century on the whole, the tradition of chastity was accepted, though it was often violated, rebelled against and flouted. Unchastity had an added piquancy from its rebellious character. Today when it is no longer shocking, the thrill has to be more and more manufactured; so writers and publishers of salacious sexual literature do a good trade.

This situation means that the Christian teaching on chastity can no longer be merely declared; it has to be justified; it has to commend itself, because most people will not take the Bible or the Church as authoritative. The Bible and the Church did not earlier have to give reasons for their insistence on chastity; they simply announced it as the will of God or as the right kind of behaviour for members of the Christian community. You will find the Biblical material fully set out in William Graham Cole's volume: *Sex and Love in the Bible.*[2]

By the way, the Bible has not added the prohibition of sexual licence to the morals of mankind. Unrestricted sexual behaviour has almost universally been discouraged and punished, especially when adulterous. There are of course deviations. In many tribes premarital sex play occurs with approval. There is the practice of lending a wife to a visitor as part of hospitality. And relaxations of restraints in ceremonial orgies testify that normally intercourse is confined to marriage. Sex relations have always been hedged about with regulations.[3]

The Old Testament has a strict sexual code. It seems to have been more lenient to fornication on the part of the male than to the female, for obvious reasons of pregnancy. To the condemnation of adultery, which is a social as well as a moral offence, it has added proscription of all extra-marital sexual relations. It restricts sexual opportunity for economic, tribal and cultural reasons; and on top of these, it places a moral and religious factor which overrides them all. It connects sex restrictions with loyalty to the true God and separation from the heathen. The heathen were for the Israelites those who belonged to the old Canaanitish religion with its fertility rites, worship of mother earth and dithyrambic sexual licence, parallel to the Dionysian cults of Thrace which invaded Greece. But along with the Old Testament's strict sexual code, which was the mark of the chosen people in contrast to surrounding peoples, there is no denigration of sexual experience and pleasure as such, no prudish or squeamish embarrassment about it. The close association made by the Old Testament prophets between *unchastity* and unfaithfulness to the covenant with the Lord, has its basis in the fact that the surrounding peoples held a religion in which man is part of society, society is part of nature and nature is divine. Therefore communion with the divine is by immersion in the stream of nature, and the quickest way to the stream of nature is through sex. The Bible stridently contradicts this picture. Nature is not the mediator between God and man. God is nature's creator, He stands behind it. The Heavens declare the glory of God—but they are not He. And man has links with the Eternal God directly through being made in God's image; then man is lord over nature under God; he is the mediator between God and the creation—in a sense. He confronts nature with resources not derived from it. This is the world view which has led to the mastery of nature in those parts of the world which have inherited the Judaeo-Christian outlook. Mastery of nature means a mastery of sex. That is the meaning of the Old Testament's restriction of sexual experience; it is part of the covenant between Israel and the transcendent God who 'sitteth above the water floods'.

When we turn to the New Testament we find one similarity to and one big difference from the Old

Testament interpretation of chastity. The similarity is that in the New Testament too, chastity is the mark of those in the Christian covenant with God. Christ does not say much about fornication as distinct from adultery. He takes the Jewish law for granted. He says to the rich young ruler, "Thou knowest the commandments." These include "Thou shalt not commit adultery." And Christ brings this prohibition to bear completely upon husband and wife alike. Neither, if he or she is a disciple, shall put away their husband or wife and marry another (Mark x. 11, 12) and He rests this upon the Genesis announcement that from the beginning of creation God made male and female, and that in marriage they became one flesh.

This idea that man and woman become one flesh in the sexual embrace is taken up by St. Paul in his treatment of sexual relations. Whatever meaning we may give to it, it seems to signify that venereal union brings about a deep, hidden bond which is irrevocable. Because of this even intercourse with a harlot has a profound psychic effect which puts the offender out of the way of achieving a true one-flesh relation with a wife—and is therefore in contradiction with nuptial mating between disciples. The Epistles and the Acts make quite clear that fornication is forbidden. The analogy (in 1 Corinthians vi.) of fornication or adultery with the worship of false gods, implies a connection between chastity and discipleship. A review of the New Testament material suggests that the avoidance of extra-nuptial sex relations, though of older origin, is part of Christian dedication. Such chastity is an offering. Marriage is not to be regarded as a half-way house between celibacy and unrestrained wantonness, a sort of concession within severe limits to the sex urge which cannot be completely overcome because of human weakness. This concessive view is one of the widespread misrepresentations of New Testament sex doctrine encouraged by a host of modern writers, who read into the New Testament what is called the hellenistic and oriental dualism which denigrates sexual love and marriage. St. Paul, who is held to be the troublemaker in this respect and is believed to have warned against marriage because of sex, in fact commends its renunciation in his followers because marriage can be a nuisance, a distraction and a snare to worldliness, not from any doctrine that sex as such is the flesh to be overcome. There is a cryptic passage in 1 Corinthians vi. 18: "Flee fornication. Every sin that a man doeth is without the body; but he that committeth fornication sinneth against his own body." The New English Translation of the New Testament renders it: "Every other sin that a man can commit is outside the body, but the fornicator sins against his own body—for your body is a shrine of the indwelling Holy Spirit." The most likely interpretation is that while other sins are performed on the initiative of the spirit using the body as an instrument, this one, fornication, affects the body—for soul and body are closely intertwined. It affects the self in a way which cannot be undone. Mr. Cole puts it this way: "Stolen goods can be returned or compensated for, lies can be retracted and corrected, covetousness can be overcome.

33

Even idolatry can be undone and forgiven. But the sex act once committed with another person cannot be undone. The inter-personal relation has undergone a radical change, and the couple concerned can never return to where they were before. Something indelible has stamped them both".[4] Whether this perception is fully correct or not, the passage quite plainly assumes an intimate relation in St. Paul's mind between the inner life (soul) and the body, and this answers those who maintain that Christianity has made havoc of the sex problem by dissociating soul and body. The conflict between the spirit and the flesh is altogether another matter.

To summarise the New Testament sex doctrine which, we must note, is incidental rather than systematic: The Christian standard which proscribes extra-nuptial venereal experience is a pretty strict sex ethic; one that is to be observed as a vocation, one which requires suppression of strong impulses to go outside marriage for gratification. Here we see the contrast between the New Testament and the Old. In the New, chastity is a personal vocation, not merely a social and collective badge. This standard has some of the characteristics of 'the good soldier' (2 Timothy ii. 3f) who endures hardship. I am sure the non-Christian will respond more readily to this view, or at least understand it, namely the view that the Christian standard of chastity is a strict one and can only really be maintained in connection with the sense of vocation and discipleship. Outsiders, I say, will understand or respect it better than they will the patter which assumes it to be easy and just decent or respectable and which puts down all extra-marital sex behaviour as a particularly corrupt manifestation of original sin.

Restriction of venereal experience to marriage then is to be regarded, in Christian sex ethics, as one mode of Christian vocation, just as celibacy is a stricter one. Celibacy is not just bachelordom and spinsterdom, chosen because one is made that way, or inevitable for lack of opportunity to marry. Celibacy requires the suppression of all sexual experience and marriage the suppression of some. The word 'suppression' will arouse indignation in many quarters today, where the dreadful results of suppression have been put in a lurid light by the popularisation of psycho-analysis. But 'suppression' of desires is constantly practised in other spheres besides that of sex, without the bogy of mental disturbances we are warned against. Sexual desires are of course more inherent in human beings than many other desires. Yet history, and not only Christian history, provides a lot of examples of people who have 'suppressed' the impulse of Venus in the cause of some very devoted kind of life. Suppression, especially when backed by devotional, emotional and heroic ideal aids (and if the term is still allowed, sublimation) is not an inhuman achievement if undertaken deliberately and whole-heartedly. 'Suppression' in the case of sex whether it is called for by a strong sense of mission to a cause—or accepted as a vocation after it has been in-evitably laid upon us, as for those who cannot marry—this suppression must not be confused with half-hearted and reluctant *repression*, which looks over the shoulder regretting what it has missed. Such *repression* is always harmful spiritually and psychologically too.

Now, we have to look at a feature of early Christian history which baffles and disturbs many who know about it, and provides ammunition for critics who hold that the Christian influence on sexual life has been calamitous. It is the period from the second century until well into the Middle Ages, where sex is regarded as an enemy of the spirit, where virginity is exalted, where there is a flight from erotic love and from all earthly ties, where woman was held to be the embodiment of sex and the mediatrix of damnation. Mr. Sherwin Bailey in his book *Sexual Relation in Christian Thought* has collected with great scholarly industry the patristic writings which expound this flight from and fear of sexuality as a hindrance to salvation.[5] It was most vehement in the first four centuries. Christians are urged to renounce eros and venus—and domestic ties for the sake of the Kingdom of God. Celibacy was acclaimed as the best state for the Christian apostle and disciple. Origen even castrated himself in a literal following of the Lord's blessing upon those who had made themselves eunuchs for the Kingdom of God's sake.

How are we to estimate this phenomenon? You can put it down to a collective neurosis, or to the Church leaders being infected with hellenistic and oriental ideas about the evil of created and material things. There was certainly such an infiltration from pagan sources. But it is well to notice that the world of late antiquity itself had produced these manichean and gnostic schools which despised the body and its powers, because of a sense of doom upon a declining culture, and this declining culture had been marked by a sterile and feverish eroticism against which the manichean and gnostic movements reacted. One should not read the early Fathers' fury against sexuality without reading the accounts from pagan sources themselves of the brutal lasciviousness of the pagan world in the waning years of the imperial Graeco-Roman civilisation. While there *is* an element of hysteria about this, it is not all abnormal. We must remember that the Early Church was engaged in a warfare. I am not referring to the persecutions of the Christians, but to the whole character of the Church militant in carrying out the mastery of man over the stream of Nature, which mastery he was commanded to exercise in the Bible. It was a tremendous striving over the determinisms of history and over the sterility of self-love. Moreover it was a battle against the Flesh the World and the Devil. Men fled to the desert to subdue these first in themselves. Later this damming up of men's inner powers was projected´outward and after some centuries this mastery over men's earthy inheritance was turned on to the world. It then served to make history instead of just enduring it; it served to make communities engaged in education; it served to transform tribal into political organisation, to create European civic life upon the ruins of Imperial Rome. By subduing sexual powers, it wound up a spring which when uncoiled transformed sex into a highly personal thing—where love in our modern sense made its appearance. You can feel abhorrence at the ascetic crushing of natural impulses, as you can read about them in the literature of the Church from the second to the twelfth century. But the critics who will have it that it was all a disaster, do not realise, because they lack understanding of cultural history, that if this urgent asceticism had not occurred, man's power over his destiny which is such a predominant feature of European civilisation, would likewise not have taken place. There would have been no modern Europe if the sexual behaviour of early European man had been as spontaneously unrestricted as that of the natives of Samoa whose sexual freedom so enthrals Margaret Mead. We shall return to this in lecture six.

The sharp flight from sex was soon modified. Marriage took its place again in the teaching of the Church. It had all the time gone on in the populace. Even when celibacy was most prized as a weapon in religious warfare, the married state is respected even if only as a second best. After Tertullian, Gregory of Nazianzen, Chrysostom and others recognised the two states of life, Augustine who regarded sexual concupiscence as the result of the Fall, wrote his *de Bono conjugali* in which he defends marriage as an honourable estate, as against the *Manicheans* and *Gnostics* for whom it was *per se* evil. It was the devotees of these non-Christian cults who proclaimed to the uttermost the evil of all natural earthly powers, and regarded woman as the chain round man's neck, because for them feminity was the earthy as contrasted with the spiritual principle. These rivals to Christianity had brought in again the old contrast represented in Greece by Apollo and Dionysos—the heavenly virgin god and the wild untamed natural powers; they transferred it to the male and female polarity. The Christian writers are mild and sober in their battle against being overwhelmed by the flesh, compared with these heathen movements.

One other thing this period produced was a new and responsible view of virginity. It was not now an escape from the thraldom of passion, but a positive way in which sex could be canalised. The virgin man or woman is not sexless. It was the transforming of the sexual and erotic powers into non-erotic channels that made for greater resources in religious and social influence. When celibacy for the clergy was insisted on in the eleventh century, the priest was not a de-sexed man. In fact, being a eunuch was an impediment for receiving Holy Orders and required dispensation, for the priest must be a whole man with his complete virility; and by depriving his virility of its normal expression in relation with woman, he developed a feminine counterpart in himself which made him a good pastor.

In the end the idea of holy matrimony ran side by side with holy virginity. Indeed as Dr. J. V. L. Casserley has said "The idea of holy virginity is indispensable to the idea of holy matrimony."[6] Marriage can be accepted and embraced as a high vocation only in a world in which there exists some feasible and proper alternative. Some cynics have said that only because of prostitution has the marriage bond been saved. Vocation to virginity is not the same as self-satisfied bachelordom or

spinsterhood enjoyed by complacent single people—
nor is it the idealism of sour grapes for those who have
missed the married state. It is a commitment under
God, parallel to that of marriage. Without a place for
vocational virginity, sexuality and marriage become
necessary and cease to be vocational. We may say that
Christianity released man from the necessity of choos-
ing between marriage and sex on the one hand, and
promiscuous sexual behaviour on the other.

There are two other fruits of the damping down of
the sexual impulses in early Christianity, which must
be mentioned. One is the obscure way in which it later
in the fourteenth century begot (with some queer
other parentage) the invention of courtly love. This has
given the modern West a new view of eros and the
relation of the sexes. Romantic love which still provides a haze of exaltation in men and women relations,
is an outcome of the paradoxical history of sexual love
in Christian history. We will attend to this in the next
lecture.

Closely connected with it is the position of women.
The flight from sex in early Christendom was associated with a flight by men from women. Woman
was not despised so much as held in a frightening
prestige. The ladies will not mind this; there is no
woman who would not rather be regarded as dangerous
than as negligible or a mere convenience. In the long
period from the second century to the eleventh or
twelfth, the distinction between body and spirit,
nature and mind, was stretched to the limit; the body
was regarded as the enemy of the soul; all ties of the

flesh seemed evil, an attitude surviving in certain aspects of modern puritanism which equate the world the flesh and the devil with the pub, the flapper and the bookmaker. And it was the idealistic Greeks and the heroes of the spirit in Christianity, who felt that in woman lay the incarnate enemy of the light. Simone de Beauvoir writes: "But she is never left to nature: she is surrounded by taboos and purified by rites. Men and women approach one another through ceremonials and sacraments which withdraw her from the earth and the flesh and change her into a fully human creature. Whereupon the magic she exercised is canalised like the lightning conductors and power station canalise electricity. It is even possible to use her powers in the general interest, and here we see another phase in the oscillation which marks the relation of man and woman. He loves her to the extent that she is his; he fears her in so far as she remains the other; but it is as the fearsome other that he seeks to make her more profoundly his—and this is what will bring him to elevate her to the dignity of being a person and lead him to recognise in her a fellow creature."[7] Besides, outside the love relation, it was in the monastic religious houses for women, the nunneries, that women learned to organise, to do business, to exercise authority and guidance in a community, tasks which had before been regarded as masculine prerogatives. So it was Christianity paradoxically that was to proclaim on a certain plane the equality of man and woman.

We must now leave this historical sketch: and I conclude with a brief summary of the difference

Christianity has made to the sexual mores of mankind. By confining its approval to marital sexuality the Christian Church has led to sex being regarded partly as the expression, and partly the instrument of, a lifelong personal relation. The development of erotic personality becomes the background of other bonds in marriage, namely interpersonal, economic, domestic and parental bonds. This joining of several bonds does not of course make life easier, for conflicts between them inevitably arise. But beginning with the notes of responsibility and respect which seem to inform the Biblical contribution, Christendom built up the idea of fidelity, and later by adopting the courtly love element it brought romantic love into the marriage relationship at a great risk. Christendom has thus given to western man a sense that sex without marriage is a violation of full and genuine interpersonal regard.

EROS AND ROMANTIC LOVE

SEX in mankind has a dual aspect. It is on the one hand a field of experience running down into nature from the conscious activities of the spirit. I am referring of course to the human spirit by which *homo* is to some extent above the stream of nature and the processes of history, a self who confronts nature or history and some of his own inner processes. Sex is, on the other hand, the field in which nature becomes highly personalised. In sexuality, then, man is both involved in nature and also confronts it with a consciousness standing to some extent outside it. This double fact is the reason for there being an enigma of sex, that there is not for instance about digestion.

I distinguished, in my first lecture, several levels in the sexual relationships of man and woman. There is, at the basis, the sex urge, purely biological, which *homo* shares with the lower animals. In itself it is impersonal, driving the male and female of the species to unite sexually. In so far as it becomes the sole mover in human beings, one woman or one man is as good as another. But it is hardly ever thus isolated, at any rate in developed societies. Securing a sexual mate is usually accompanied by satisfactions beyond the release of a pent up instinct, such as a sense of conquest, of power, of status, of tenderness, of release by immersion in the life stream away from the more deliberate strains of mental and social discipline.

But also, more positively, in mankind as we know it, the sex urge becomes incorporated in the second level of sexuality, that is the mutual attraction of one man and one woman to each other. This is part of what we will call Eros. Eros is a longing for completeness, with the begininning of the personalisation of sex. It has of course a much wider field than that of sex. The Greeks recognised this force of *eros* as the desire to fill up a lack; it is a sort of yearning for completeness, sometimes for the possession of a definite satisfaction or object, but sometimes too for an unknown satisfaction which one is groping for. Eros is a form of 'need love' to use an expression aptly coined by Prof. C. S. Lewis in his book *The Four Loves*[1] in which he unfolds love as affection, love as friendship, love as eros, and love as charity. The chapter on Eros is on the theme of this lecture.

Plato had put into the mouth of Socrates, who claims to be reproducing the teaching of the Sibyl Diotima, the formula that eros is the child of penury (poverty) and plenitude (riches).[2] Eros is neither divine nor mortal, but that which draws them together by the poverty of mortals seeking to appropriate the riches of the divine. It includes the love of the beautiful and 'the desire for the everlasting possession of the good'. Sexual passion and love of offspring are the works of eros, but so also are mankind's striving to formulate laws, to make inventions and do noble deeds, to create

44

sciences, arts and cultures. This is all a striving for the ideal beauty and goodness or knowledge. We can see how this Platonic architecture of the works of eros came to be used in Christian ages to describe man's insatiable search for an abiding satisfaction and how this insatiableness is a sign that he is made for an infinite bliss which can only be found in union with God. St. Augustine stated eros in Christian terms when he uttered his famous saying "Thou hast made us for thyself and our heart is restless till it find rest in Thee."

In the sexual field this need love of eros is much more than the need for venereal pleasure; it contains it but goes far beyond it and sometimes finds satisfaction of the sex urge interfering with the demands of eros. In the love relation of men and women, there is not primarily the need of sex but the need of another person. In most cases people fall in love first and that brings about the desire for intimate union throughout the whole scale, from its roots in blood and earth to the most soaring of ideal dreams. Being in love is the most selfless of experiences; we are taken out of ourselves and concerned only with the other; the self that desires drops out of the picture. That is why lovers as such are humble. There is no squinting round to see oneself as desiring—it is an almost outward looking condition. Venus may be followed purely out of regard for one's own pleasure; but eros is a need not for pleasure or happiness, but for the other one. And all the poets who have sung the praises of love know that the lover knows that love may mean sorrow and pain as well as joy.

But he does not calculate which of the two, joy or sorrow, will be the greater. 'I want you', nothing else, whether it brings a crown or a cross. That is why lovers consider warnings by their elders that their love affair will lead to misery, as quite irrelevant. Young lovers spend much time saying nothing—or making inarticulate noises—for words are an interference with the one unspeakable union which only needs presence and touch. They would be away alone from everything and everybody. "If you were the only girl in the world and I were the only boy." And when they do talk it is endlessly about the other and about oneself. And in the state of being in love to talk about oneself is not egoism, for it is only egotistic to talk about oneself when the other does not want to listen. Here each wants to hear the other talk about himself or herself. When people are in love it is not sex they want, it is each other, and when the sex urge is aroused, it is felt to be something to be satisfied 'for ourselves alone'.

The Russian writer, Vladimir Solovyev, wrote a short treatise on love. In it he writes "The meaning and worth of love, as a feeling, consists in this, that it effectually constrains us, in all our nature, to acknowledge for another the unconditional central significance, of which in virtue of our egoism, we are conscious only in our own selves. Love is of importance, not only as one of our feelings, but as the transfer of all our interest (in life) from ourselves to another, as the shifting of the very centre of our personal life."[3]

I have called eros a manifestation of need-love (to

46

use Professor Lewis' expression) and indeed it is, but it is need for the other as a whole person, not for what he or she can do for us. One's need is submerged; eros attends only to the other as something admirable in his or her self. Eros thus obliterates the contrast between giving and receiving.

What draws a man and a woman into falling in love is quite unpredictable. It is a mystery—and a mystery as someone has truly said, is not a definite uncertainty but an indefinite certainty. The certainty is indefinable (though some psychologists try to explain part of it in terms of the proportion of feminine and masculine elements in each one's make-up). The certainty is that each man and each woman is drawn by the force of eros to be attracted by a certain kind of the opposite sex — and to seek the only one that fully attracts—'the soul mate' or whatever you call it. "He or she is not my type" you hear young people say. "I couldn't marry him," or "I can't see what he saw in her." And it is not some obvious quality in the other that accounts for it; Touchstone in *As You Like It* spoke of his girl Audrey "A poor thing, but mine own!"

I have, of course, isolated the condition of being in love, and tried to describe it in, as it were, its glowing colours. Eros is the principle of attraction, and it seeks to preserve the 'I and Thou' relation in its entirety and its isolation. But not only is eros never allowed un-disputed sway in actual living; there are other claims upon the person in love. Also the idyllic love relation may turn to its own overthrow—transformed even to hate when its perfection is disappointed. Furthermore,

47

if being in love leads to a permanent union, either in marriage or a long lived 'liaison amoureuse', a new factor enters in. It is the problem of 'living together'. This is the really personal level in sexual relationships. What happens here is that man and woman, drawn to each other on the two other levels of the biological sex urge and of the mutual attraction of being in love, have now to meet each other as whole persons. And as whole persons, each cannot be confined to their role as venereal partners or as meeting the need of erotic attraction. They have to learn to live as neighbours, this man and this woman, with other needs and concerns than those of venus or of eros. And they have to regard each other as neighbours who have been closely linked by the impersonal force of venereal desire and the emotional tie of being, or having been, in love. This is what makes married love an art, for it is often easier to be a good neighbour to one a little way off, than to the one you are tied to by the invisible and powerful bonds of venus and eros. The married are helped over the breakdowns of love by the institution of marriage. Many love affairs have no such help; the union depends upon each being always emotionally up to scratch—and it's an awful strain. Sometimes the long love union outside marriage, sustained by eros alone, is tolerable because the two escape the boredom of sharing the same house all the time. I knew of a Frenchman once who had the same mistress for twenty years. When his friends said "Why don't you marry her, you know you won't ever have anybody else," he replied: "Yes, that's true, but where should I go in the evenings?" Being cooped up together is galling to those who have not learned the art of living together as neighbours. On the other side, this living as neighbours between whole persons—drawn maybe by the full force of love—can be made intolerable if eros is felt to be the only bond. A distinguished lady wrote in a woman's journal not long ago, that after reading much of the advice given to the young for married happiness—after thirty years of her own marriage—"I can imagine nothing fitter to destroy it," namely married happiness, "than having a perpetual Romeo about the place."

Romantic Love has taken a decisive place in our western Christendom and still affects our way of thinking about sexuality. This specialised form of eros has its constructive and destructive side. There is the dark eros—connected with pain and the death wish—and the glowing eros which takes the attraction of man and woman into a realm of personal commitment. And Romantic Eros is a terrible tyrant; those under its sway are in danger of sacrificing all other loyalties and often the partners themselves. Just because those under the sway of romantic love lose their egoism each in concern for the other, it looks like the noblest kind of self-forgetfulness. Therein lies its danger. Let me quote again from Professor C. S. Lewis, "It is in the grandeur of Eros that the seeds of danger are concealed. He has spoken like a god. His total commitment, his reckless disregard of happiness, his transcendence of self regard, sounds like a message from the eternal world . . . And yet it cannot, just as it stands, be the voice of God himself. For Eros, speaking with that very grandeur

49

and displaying that very transcendence of self may urge to evil as well as to good . . . The love which leads to cruel and perjured unions, even to suicide pacts and murder, is not likely to be wandering lust or idle sentiment. It may well be Eros in all his splendour; heartbreakingly sincere, ready for every sacrifice except renunciation."[4] I would add ready for every sacrifice except that of acknowledging that romantic love is not supreme, as if it owed no allegiance to a higher law than its own. Professor Lewis adds two things. "Eros may unite the most unsuitable yoke fellows, many unhappy and predictably unhappy marriages were love matches," and "Of all the loves Eros is at his height the most godlike; therefore most prone to demand our worship. Of himself he always tends to turn 'being in love' into a sort of religion. The real danger seems to me not that the lovers will idolise each other but that they will idolise Eros himself."

And, now, not only has eros its dark dangerous side, it has its deceptions—for eros is the most tricky of loves. Eros tells his devotees that in it the lovers find permanence. To be in love is to reject the idea that it is transitory; it intends life-long fidelity. Yet, romantic love is actually most fickle and unpredictable. Literature is full of the dramas and tragedies when the permanence which being in love counts upon proves a cheat. "Had we never lov'd sae kindly, had we never lov'd sae blindly, never met—or never parted, we had ne'er been broken-hearted." I quote Burns from memory. Beside this kind of genuine pathos, there is the overwhelming destructive love of eros, such as that to be found in a modern novel *The Dead Seagull*, by George Barker.

We must remember that romantic love has a limited history; it is not common to mankind—at any rate not as something to be desired. You will find its history beginning in the twelfth century courtly love of Languedoc, told in Professor C. S. Lewis's *The Allegory of Love*,[5] where he points out what a new thing it was and suggests that its sway might have an end. Mario Praz gives the dark sadistic side in *The Romantic Agony*,[6] though that is more about venereal lust than about romantic love. There are some excellent chapters on the later phases in J. Huizinga's *The Waning of the Middle Ages*.[7] I think we may be seeing the end of romantic love now, even in the Anglo-Saxon countries where it has survived longest as an ideal. There are few romanticists of love among contemporary fiction writers, and they are mostly elderly. The very modern writers picture sexual love as a kind of dreary dead craving, like the craving to go on smoking which one doesn't enjoy, merely because one would feel bereft without it. Much contemporary sex in literature depicts sexuality as cut off not only from all morality, which is regarded as 'uncivilised', but also cut off from love in any thrilling sense. Miss Iris Murdoch's book *The Severed Head* is a good example.

The origins of 'courtly love' are disputed. One account traces it to social causes, in a relatively settled world and district where men were many and women few in the castles of the knightly gentry. De Rougemont in *l'Amour et l'Occident*[8] finds its sources in the infiltration of Manichaean and Cathar influences into Southern France—and he regards the whole thing as a rival to Christianity. Be this as it may, the elements of it are the knight's fidelity to a lady whom he did not seek in marriage, a devotion to her who was often another man's wife. It is the frustration of unfulfilled love that gives it its zest. This romantic offering of loyalty and fidelity to one woman when it remained true to the original idea, would come to an end if it resulted in marriage or sexual union with the beloved. Of course there were many adulteries; but on the whole it was the distance between the lover and his lady that preserved the force of *amour courtois*. All this produced a mixture of humility, courtesy, fidelity, in the relations of men and women of a restricted class, with of course its frequent breakdowns and an unhealthy trend to make a religion of love. The image of death is never far away—and the tragic side of romantic love emerges in western literature, typified by the Tristan and Isolde theme. Also it produced a new kind of equality between men and women. Out of it arose a most highly perfected image of woman.

By the end of the fourteenth century this kind of romantic love began to be thought of as possible and right within marriage. Father Gervaise Mathew O.P. has described this development in *Marriage and Amour Courtois in late Fourteenth Century England*.[9] He paraphrases an Anglo-Norman allegory on such love in marriage. "Love is a naked boy, yellow haired and blind. He holds a dart and roses fly from him like sparks. His castle is raised on loyalty and its keep is a loyal heart. His three enemies are Mistrust and Treason and their father Falsehood, while jealousy is the mangonel with which they attempt to breach his castle wall. He who loves worthily must be loyal and have a loyal heart. He must have courtesy and always speak courteously. He must know all women and always speak well of them. He must be able to keep his own counsel and to keep chaste and to keep his mind from *lecherie et ordure,* and if his love is answered he will know himself to be unworthy and will do all things to increase the pleasure and honour of her who has answered it. They will take each other in holy church. But being married they remain *amys et amye* and such good loving rightly used can please and serve God and bring them to a joy without end."

The mutual service and honour of husband and wife are in this literature expressed in the terms of courtly love. They marry and have children and after marriage are still described as lovers. *The Knighte's Tale* is quoted as expressing this sentiment:

> "and thus with alle blisse and melodye
> Hath Palamon y-wedded Emelye . . .
> And Emelye him loveth so tendrely
> And he hir serveth al so gentilly."

While courtly love permeated the marriage bond and moved from being a purely knightly ideal to one shared by the burgher class, its language also coloured the religious literature of the time. As early as the twelfth century St. Bernard had used this language to describe man's love for God. Then St. Francis called himself one of God's troubadours, and said he had a most glorious and gracious lady and her name was Poverty. The Blessed Henry Suso conceived the saint as a huntsman and a warlike knight, and the entry to paradise as like being dubbed Knight of God for valour, whose most prized virtue was undying constancy. Dante had been nurtured in the literature of courtly love. His lady Beatrice was neither his wife nor his mistress. The real young woman of the *Vita Nuova* became in the *Divine Comedy* the earthly type of the love of God. Miss Dorothy L. Sayers describes Dante's love for her as follows: "Of all the loves he had known—and the witness, internal and external, is that he had known love in many kinds, including 'the dark Eros' and the '*debito amore*' (the love which is due between husband and wife)—this (his love for Beatrice) is the one which, with will and judgment assenting, he declares to be a revelation of divine truth. It is not the febrile anguish of the death-Eros, in which possession for ever mocks desire; nor yet the simple and affectionate exchange which does not look beyond possession. It is in fact not concerned with possession one way or the other, though it may survive loss. It is a love whose joy—and therefore its fulfilment—consists in the worshipful contemplation of that which stands over and above the worshipper. True to its origins in courtly love, it finds its entire happiness in being allowed to do homage to its acknowledged superior."[10]

All this tradition of romantic love is a limited phenomenon both locally and historically. It is a feature of our western culture. It links sex with affection and with personal enhancement of the love partner. Among primitive men this is not so; affection is there a bond between kinsfolk and has no necessary connection with sex and marriage. Briffault testifies to the greater disposition to whole-hearted, if perhaps less deep and constant, affection in primitive society than in modern man. "Primitive man," he writes, "is as prone as civilised man to sensual desire; he is equally capable of tender affection; what is unknown to him is the intimate combination of the two."[11]

Western notions of love with their individualised and idealised form of sex relationship do not occur in the East. Instead of our problem of Eros and Agape, which are part of our inheritance in Christendom, the East has a wider doctrine of compassion, especially in Buddhism. In the ancient classical world something like romantic love was recognised, but it was regarded as an affliction, a temporary insanity. Lucretius has an eloquent passage about its deceptions.[12]

We have looked backward for a moment from the Mediaeval upsurge of romantic love. Now to take a jump nearer to our own day, and to overlook the Elizabethan period which manifested some of the feeling of torment in the destructive character of love, we find a new turn in the eighteenth century. Then romantic love became one of the bemusing inspirations of Anglo-Saxon civilisation, and this was a kind of compensation for the loss of man's integration in society and work and for boredom in utilitarian and predominantly economic pursuits. This conception of individualised romantic love as the great adventure of life culminating in marriage was a kind of counter-weight to the uprooting of mankind from its social soil in the early period of the commercial and industrial revolution. To quote from a well known sociologist. "In its idealising quality and in its tendency to ignore or sublimate the sexual aspect it resembles the older chivalry; in its concentration upon an exclusive object of devotion and particularly in its implication that marriage is the adventurous goal of the attachment, it is far apart from that principle."[13]

Several anthropologists and sociologists have called attention to the modern American situation where romantic love and its ideal in marriage co-exist with the largest experimentation in divorce and re-marriage. "The hero of the modern American movies is always a romantic lover just as the hero of the old Arab epic is always an epileptic."[14] To quote another observer: "The forms of love are today peculiarly fused into the vision of a single person of the opposite sex, at once sacred and profane, of this world and the next, desired supremely for a permanent attachment called marriage. Such a love offers nothing so much as an island of hope where two, at least, in a world raked by rivalry and dark with indifference, can ever be true to each other."[15]

These are the dreams of romantic love today. Perhaps the inability of people to rise to the dream's require-ments should be included in the causes of family breakdown. But the dream itself must, I think, be taken as a desire for an area of personal fulfilment and human security in a calculating, anxious, go-getting civilisation, as it was for Matthew Arnold when he wrote *Dover Beach*.

And yet, it is in just this climate, suffused with romantic love as the ideal, which most easily encourages the idea of marriage as a contract to be broken when the hope dies, and of experimenting again with new partners. This I regard as the worst marriage system in the world. Lest you should think that this is a miserable masculine devaluation of romance, I add that, as we shall see later, romantic love is a masculine invention.

We return, in conclusion, to more prosaic analysis. We are engaged in an examination of the sexual relation of man and woman, in order to understand that this sexual relation involves both conflict and possible harmony between these three levels of sexuality. They are sex urge (venus), the emotional attachments (eros) and the meeting of the partners as neighbours. This will draw the subject, including eros, within the framework of Christian Sex Ethics. To state the matter briefly now, it is just this. Failures in one level bring disasters in the other levels. Firstly, the search for pure sensual pleasure in venereal experiment *à la* Lucretius or Casanova, in which any man or woman will do, impairs the capacity of the man or woman for that one-to-one personal attachment which is falling in love. Lucretius openly acknowledged that being in love spoiled the pleasure of venus. Secondly, the calamities of eros and of living together and strains in relation of lovers as persons, react upon venereal experience. This is ignored by much guidance offered young people:

it assumes that what is most needed is knowledge of the techniques of venereal pleasure and sexual intercourse. I will explain later how breakdowns in the love life of lovers and the neighbour in marriage distort the venereal relation, and often make chastity especially difficult.

The third way in which the three levels interact is, of course, that marriages break down or are rendered ghastly, and infidelity is excused, because the partners have relied upon the bonds of venus and eros only, and never learned to live as neighbours. The idea is that if love in the romantic sense fails or dies then the marriage too has died and had better be ended. They have never learned any other kind of love beside that of romantic eros. To the reconciliation of the three levels in marriage we turn in the next lecture.

4

THE MARRIAGE COVENANT

WHEN a man and a woman marry they bring into their new relationship three factors which have drawn them together. They are the sex urge (venus); the mutual attraction (eros) and each one's own individuality. In the marriage relationship they then acquire three responsibilities, namely to maintain the social and legal status of the marriage, the co-operative task of running a household, and in most cases the rearing of children. These acquired tasks modify the bare 'you' and 'I' relationship. It is in the carrying out of these acquired tasks that the partners learn to know one another not just as man or woman, not merely as lovers, but as neighbours. I shall elaborate later how some of the problems of marriage derive mostly from failure in this level, namely in the contact of two neighbours who are linked together by the intimate bonds of venereal union and by mutual attraction or being in love. This is important because breakdowns in marriage are often mistakenly attributed entirely to failure in the other two levels, either to ignorance of the arts and techniques of venereal love, or to the waning of a romantic attachment.

We have noted that the biological sex urge itself is impersonal and anonymous. It draws any male and female to unite bodily. At the level of eros—and especially that form of eros we call being in love—there enters a highly personal factor. 'This one you and this one I' want one another. But though personalised it is not what we may call the meeting of two persons conscious of their own individuality. The germs of individuality are of course there, for people express their erotic love differently, but each one's own individuality is for the time being submerged. Consciousness is given only to the other. There are of course breaks in this blissful loss of one's own individuality; the individuality of one or both is brought into consciousness when a threat is detected in the behaviour of the other. Hence the lovers' quarrels and sometimes a real or feigned gesture of withdrawal. "If you go on like that, it's off." But so long as being in love goes on unbroken—and when its rupture is mended—the individuality of each is out of sight. We may say that erotic love is the reverse of insistence on one's individuality. Also that it believes in its own permanence; and again that it is self-contained, indifferent to what the world around does about it.

Marriage is the institutionalised expression of the belief that the erotic relationship will be permanent. It is therefore the fulfilment of the most personalised impulse in the state of being in love. But the other two features of the condition of 'being in love' can never be permanent—namely the submerging of each one's individuality and the mental exclusion of the outside world. Husband and wife find that in the marriage bond their bodily union and their mutual attraction have to be accommodated with these two other facts which could be overlooked in the 'being in love' condition. To repeat, the two facts are that man or woman is not only a male and female, not only a lover and beloved, but also a person with an individuality and purposes other than that of being a love partner; and secondly that this personal bond has to be geared to the social relation of both and each. Now *homo* is both an individual and a social being—married or not. If the love relation crushes either the individuality of one or both, or extinguishes his other social contacts, it stops the full personal development of one or other or both.

This is the rationale of marriage as the field for completing the personalisation of the whole being, which runs from the pulsation of the life stream, the sensual delights of mutual bodies, the emotional surge of personal love, the meeting of the partners with other men and women, the work each has to do, the common interests, and the separate interests. All this is about what we may call 'marriage in the order of nature', quite apart from its legal aspects and apart from religious interpretations. Marriage in Christianity is not a different kind of marriage. Christian marriage, or Holy Matrimony, sets this natural marriage in another dimension and places all these complex relationships in a new depth. Those who enter the state of Holy Matrimony with awareness, do not add on religion as an extra, but see the whole scale of their love relation as under God. What that means I leave until a little later.

I think it is possible now to understand the significance of the marriage vow. A vow is one of the most direct acts of personal responsibility and decision. The sex urge and falling in love are not deliberate decisions, but so that the sex urge and being in love shall minister to the growth of full personal stature they are included in a decision that the bond they create shall be permanent. And because marriage leads to families, and families are ingredients of the social order, the state has a right to recognise it as such. Hence the legal aspects of the marriage covenant.

Marriage is a state of life entered into by the consenting parties. It gives status to a bond which, if left only to the waywardness of the sex urge or to the brittleness of being devotedly in love, would break down over and over again. And unless it is recognised as a status, it cannot fulfil the full personal relationship which we have outlined. You know the difference between a status and an agreement or contract. A status is something on which you can count, like being a child in a family, or a citizen. The child has a status in the home. He or she has a natural claim to a certain treatment and affection because they belong there. There are ties and givings and receivings quite apart from what he or she earns by behaviour. He does not have to buy his privileges by what he does. The inmate of a home may feel sore, injured, rebellious, resentful and wilful; but unless he cuts right away, he knows all the time that whatever he may or may not do, he will have to come round in the end, because the ties that bind him are not external actions but his very nature which is of one substance with that of his family. By contrast, an agreement can be terminated, a contract can be cancelled, like the tenancy of a house or a wage bargain. Many human relations in civilisation are contractual, but there has to be somewhere in which a human being is regarded for what he is and not just for what he does.

In marriage a man or woman enters voluntarily into a new status, like, but different from, the status they enjoyed as the young of their original families. To have some part of our life as a status is paradoxically a condition of freedom; because human beings, not being pure spirits, must have settlement in some part of their existence in order to be free in others. If you have a lever you are free to lift many heavy things, but only because you yourself are not free from the pull of the earth's gravity. You can count on that, to stop you being rocketed into outer space.

So the wisdom of Christendom —and to a large extent the human race itself—has placed the relation of the sexes in that layer of existence which is one of status. That is the human meaning of the status of marriage. The status of marriage, however, is not naturally given, like a child's membership of its family, or the status one has as a citizen by being born in England. Men and women take on the status of marriage by an act of consent.

But notice what this consent implies. In our western marriage law it is consent between two persons to engage in the status of marriage. The consent is formally embodied in a contract of marriage, in church or before a registrar. John takes Mary to his wedded wife, and Mary takes John to her wedded husband. In the registry offices of this land the contracting parties are informed that by the law of England marriage is a lifelong union of one man and one woman to the exclusion of all others. This is not abrogated by the fact of the state now claiming under certain circumstances to dissolve the marriage by divorce decrees. The point to grasp here is that whatever powers the legislature may take to dispense from the obligation of the marriage state, this power to dispense with allowance to re-marry, does not imply as is widely believed, that marriage is a contract. The contract is one to enter into a state. You will find this succinctly put in T. A. Lacey's *Marriage in Church and State*, where it is explained that the state of marriage is not a contractual relation, the bond is not a contractual bond.[1] The contract is only the instrument by which the state of matrimony is brought about. It is not a continuing contract subject to revision, or capable of being rescinded with due regard for law by agreement of the parties interested. It is completed by consummation. Thenceforward the relationship of the parties is determined, not by contract, but by law, divine and human, recognising the new status. The married pair are bound to the fulfilment of their mutual duties, not by their own consent but by a natural obligation, that is, one inherent in the new status. It is an obligation to live together for life in a perfect union of equal partnership for the procreation and nurture of children, for mutual support and comfort in good and evil estate, and for the right ordering of the family.

This conception of marriage which underlies our matrimonial jurisdiction—even though the conception is broken into by legalised divorce facilities—has its origin in the ecclesiastical law of earlier times. The Church however stated it as the law of marriage in the natural order; that is to say, it represented the essential *natura* or essence of marriage. Christian marriage or Holy Matrimony does not add to the conception but brings out its religious implications. You will find this briefly set forth in a recently published sermon by the Revd. G. R. Dunstan *The Marriage Covenant*.[2] He there elaborates the parallelism between the status of marriage shared by two persons, and the covenant relation between God and Israel in the Old Testament, and between Christ and His Church in the New. "An *initiative* of love wins a response, and creates a relationship of status. This covenant once initiated is made permanent by an oath. The vow is the moral assent of the man and of the woman, the engaging of their whole rational selves to what the heart dictates." The covenant has its commandments. First, "mutual subjection in love, mutual care seeking the good of the beloved". The second commandment is fidelity. Then, besides the commandments are the promises of the covenant: the power to keep the commandments of the covenant, and the grace of forgiveness when they are broken. "The two do become one and 'signify', or exemplify, to the world the mystical union that is betwixt Christ and His Church." The last mark of the covenant is sacrifice, for marriage requires it, whether it is understood religiously or not. But where the sacrifice is not consciously accepted and embraced, but allowed to fester in the dormitories of the soul with resentment, the state of matrimony is marred. Marriage involves "a death to dependence of childhood upon father and mother; a death to bachelor and spinster freedoms, a death to certain rights of self-determination," to one's own way and one's own pleasures, and also to the giving pleasure to the other in one's own way.

An American journal once gave advice that when a man marries he should realise that he is giving up fifty per cent of his independence. When the late G. K. Chesterton read it he exclaimed, "That is of course another splendid example of transatlantic optimism." He knew more than most men the paradoxal truth that sacrifice of aggressive self-dependence in marriage brings a new kind of personal freedom, as his love poems testify, the freedom of a militant enterprise, sure of victory. Listen to this from his *Marriage Song*:

"We break the line with stroke and luck,
The arrows run like rain,
If you be struck or I be struck,
There's one to strike again.
If you befriend, or I befriend,
The strength is in us twain
And good things end and bad things end,
And you and I remain."

The sacrifices involved in marriage were symbolised in earlier rituals by gifts to each other, and they have still their masquerading ghost in the wedding breakfast or reception. Besides these greater sacrifices inherent in marriage, there is also involved a sacrifice in the bearing of pain, the boring pain of living with the irritating little habits of the other partner, the stinging pain of wounded love, pain in forgiveness for deep injury and pain in the loss of the loved one by death.

We shall examine in more concrete detail the problems of living together by man and wife, in the next lecture. Now we will see what the Church means by Holy Matrimony. Holy Matrimony is natural marriage seen in the context of man's relation to God. This is not to say that marriage between Christians has to be informed all the time by religious considerations. It is to say that each partner knows and affirms to himself and herself, and sometimes to the other, that their relationship and the family are God given and God blessed. Especially that he and she have been given to each other by divine decree, and that they see one another as persons whom God has drawn to consent in wedlock, through the fact of sex, mutual attraction and the personal decision to enter the marriage status. All this is a certain background of awareness; it does not demand a fully conscious attention all the time. Just as one can have a hidden sense that one is doing a job of work for the Lord while one's conscious attention is rightly on the job, for it would be wrong to be mooning about devotionally; and as one consciously offers one's nourishment as a gift of God when we say grace and then rightly proceed to enjoy one's dinner with our mind on that, so we can repeatedly recall our marriage as something to which we are called by God, without supposing that we must be prayerful in the marriage bed or in the household tasks or in the social intercourse with children and friends or in the recreations we take. If we are practising our religion by public worship, by our private prayer life, and by the outstanding moments when we bring our marriage relation (beginning with the vows at the wedding) before God, in the moments of perplexity when we want His guidance, the times of trouble when we desperately need His support, and, what is too often forgotten, when we make a glad offering of gratitude for times of great joy and happiness—then we can be genuinely certain that the whole of our married state is lived as unto God, while in most of it our minds and feelings are on what we are doing without being consciously devotional.

I leave on one side for the present an even more profound way in which a person by finding his or her life in God, becomes a better partner in neighbourhood or marriage. At the moment we are looking at the covenant of marriage itself. The Anglican Prayer Book and a number of other formularies speak of the three causes for which marriage was ordained—namely the procreation of children, the avoidance of fornication and the mutual society, help and comfort that the one ought to have of the other. People now consider the second of these rather coarse and negative; so our revised Anglican Prayer Book of 1928 replaces it by "in order that the natural instincts and affections implanted by God may be hallowed and directed aright". I think the blunt realism of the sixteenth century is much the better version. It only looks negative because we mistake the word 'causes' for 'reasons'. Few people entering upon the nuptial covenant would give any other *reason* for doing so, than that they were in love and wanted each other for good. The 'causes' mentioned are not the things *for* which they want to marry, except perhaps the third, but even that is understood rather than explicit. These things are not the reasons or motives for Robert marrying Rosalind; they are declarations to Robert and Rosalind and the public witnesses, that what they are embarking upon out of love and attraction has a certain character which belongs to the very nature of marriage. These things: begetting of offspring, sexual fidelity and mutual society and help—are not purposes of marriage so much as essentials of its nature.

Augustine had a slightly different threefold formula, *proles, fides, sacramentum*—namely procreation of offspring, fidelity, and—how shall I translate *sacramentum*?[3] It is not exactly what we mean by a *sacrament* 'an outward and visible sign of an inward and spiritual grace' though it can include that. 'Sacramentum' is in Augustine the Latin rendering of the term 'mystery' in Ephesians v. 32 at the end of the discourse on marriage —where marriage is spoken of as the two becoming one flesh. 'This mystery is great' like that of the oneness between Christ and His Church. It has the meaning of a secret, a hidden purpose of God—not seen outwardly unless it is deliberately revealed. I think we can speak of the sacramental view of marriage in this way. In Holy Matrimony Robert and Rosalind give themselves to each other utterly and completely for their whole life, in such a way that it puts down deep roots and grows into the full personal development of each. And, as Christians believe, they have their very being grounded in God who is their source as well as their end. Personality cannot flower to the full without this religious dimension. Neither is his or her own, and neither is completely the other's, for each has a godly destiny to fulfil. Dr. Casserley writes: "To be consciously married in this sense is to possess within the narrow orbit of one's own existence a vivid and pregnant analogy to our relationship to God. It is of all earthly and temporal experiences the one that most closely resembles the spiritual life, the one that best trains us in that inward and spiritual technique of self-giving which the Christian life demands."[4]

And this result cannot be fulfilled except in a union which is not broken except by death. In the light of Holy Matrimony the lifelong union is not a matter of sticking to one another because it is respectable, but of the union of two walking images of God, bringing their sexuality, their common concerns, their quarrels and reconciliations, their care of children and others into the orbit of the divine action. If marriage is to fulfil its function in the personalising of the union of man and woman, even when it is not seen in this religious context by them, it is still true that repetitive marriage with new partners after divorce is bound to spoil the personal result. This is because the marriage union is a status, with deep roots in the sexual level and an intertwining of mental, social and spiritual purposes on top of it. You don't start from scratch again when you go through a form of marriage when your former husband or wife is still alive. You carry with you the indelible marks of your former union. I say this knowing all about hard cases, and knowing some re-marriages after divorce which are relatively happy. But I know too how the failures which have wrecked one marriage are not left behind but carried into the new one.

For the same kind of reasons as I have advanced for lifelong fidelity, the status of marriage is also impaired by venereal experiment before marriage. It is often argued, especially by the misguided who think that marriage difficulties always arise in the marriage bed owing to inexperience in the arts of love, that it would make for success if the partners had some experience beforehand and knowledge of the opposite sex and their genital propensities, and had learnt some dexterity in physical love making. If this sounds so sensible to you, think what it means. It means that Robert who subsequently marries Rosalind, has been in bed with Helen. Helen knows that she is there as a sort of sparring partner in order to give him practice and improve his form for the benefit of another woman, Rosalind.[5] You can reverse the situation; and in either case you can say, if you like, what a mutual benefit would result. But, you see, it means that one of the essential ingredients of married love is destroyed, namely that it shall be with one's wife or husband that one learns the secrets of venus, and discovers each one's own intimacies. The act of sexual intercourse has since ancient times been described as 'knowing'. Adam knew his wife, and she conceived. This is a profound symbol of a real fact. In the sexual embrace a man and woman 'know' each other in a unique depth; it is the stripping off of all reserves and the opening of hidden mysteries. Therefore, if marriage is deprived of this initiation by the partners having learnt their sexual expertise with others beforehand, an essential element is lacking to the marriage experience. If people experience the act of venereal union outside marriage, either for alleged experimental skill or to express trivial and passing emotions, or for fun, or in order to appear uninhibited and sophisticated, then you render the act less capable of being the root of married love: it ceases to be the expression of true personal union between man and wife. As Bishop Mortimer puts it, "It is like using a razor to sharpen a pencil with. You sharpen your pencil all right, but you cannot later shave."[6]

I have now tried to say what the marriage covenant is; to show that the status of marriage is impaired unless it is known to be, and not merely intended, a lifelong union, and that its nature as a full meeting of two whole persons is violated by venereal adventures before or outside marriage.

We have now to relate this to the love relation and the task of living together. Failures in these two often make fidelity to the marriage covenant very difficult.[7]

5

LIVING TOGETHER

THE trouble about offering guidance to people on the art of living is that it has to be so much in terms of the problems they face and of how to deal with the problems. Life therefore looks much more complicated than it really is. Advice is often so plentiful that those who listen to it feel they will end up like the caterpillar in the poetic fable who got along quite well until it was explained to him how he walked, putting his large number of feet forward each at just the right time. The attempt to keep the rules consciously completely paralysed him, and he ended dying on his back.

Fully aware of this danger of making problems where there are not any, I nevertheless proceed to speak of the art of living together on the part of those who marry. I am of course a very small voice amid a vast torrent of guidance offered in hundreds of books and magazine articles. Here it is for what it's worth.

A new kind of relationship is entered upon when a man and woman who have been drawn together by the sex urge and a love attachment embark upon the state of marriage. I have called this new relationship that of living together as neighbours. But it is a kind of neighbourliness quite on its own, just because it contains both venus and eros; also because unless disaster occurs, it is for keeps; also because each now has to reckon on the other's preoccupations, no longer confined to the bare I-you relation; and in most cases the pristine 'you and I' meeting becomes merged in a 'we' attitude attending to common tasks and new emotional attachments to children. In addition each has to accommodate the social and friendly relations of the partner to his or her world outside marriage—friends, neighbourhood, clubs, place of work and so on. All this has in a way been lost sight of when they were merely in love. Lovers meet each other as lovers, now they have to meet as total human beings. This demands growth of a new kind of love. Married love need not extinguish eros, though it often does and then it looks drab and prosy in comparison with romance. If the longing which is the very nature of eros is not sought outside the marriage when it feels cheated inside—then marriage itself, having stripped away the haze and paint which glorified romance, gives rise to the new romance of discovering ever new and unsuspected secrets of the inner being of one's husband or wife. This disclosure is not always pleasant, but in that case if it is seen as a challenge and a discovery, the romance of marriage need never end. For in the last resort even a lifelong partner remains in some degree an inscrutable mystery. The fatal thing is to try to destroy the mystery either by a claim to completely understand the other, or to mould the other one to fit one's own capacity of understanding.

What are we to call this new kind of love, in

marriage? Our English language is poor in words for different kinds of love. The ancients had many more. One of them *agape* is the supreme kind of love in the New Testament. Some of you may be acquainted with a recent theological debate started by the Swedish theologian Nygren in a book called *Agape and Eros*.[1] Briefly his thesis was that *agape* is entirely 'gift love' to use Professor C. S. Lewis' term, and *eros* is entirely 'need love'. Nygren's argument was that eros is human and agape divine love. Only God can love with agape for He has no needs; man cannot love God or his neighbour with agape, because human love is always in need of something (even if it is only the need to be needed as in an over-possessive mother or wife who looks on the surface so helpless, but underneath craves to be wanted and resents it when she isn't). Nygren's thesis has a good deal of insight, but it has been criticised. Denis de Rougemont in *Passion and Society* has offered a quite different account of eros —and then both Nygren and de Rougemont were carefully examined and found fault with, in a great book by Father Martin D'Arcy, S.J., *The Mind and Heart of Love*.[2] A contribution to the discussion was made in John Burnaby's study of Augustine, *Amor Dei*.[3]

Nygren's sharp contrast between agape and eros is not, as a fact, true to the New Testament, where the term agape is used for earthly loves as well as for God's love for man, and even for wrong loves as in the phrase love 'not the world'. But still, there is a difference between *agape* and *eros*. Eros is search for the lovable, the attractive, it depends on some enticing quality in the object loved or believed to be in the loved object. Agape depends on no admirable quality in the loved one, it is given to the unlovable — it depends only on the loving nature of the loving subject. St. Paul describes the agape of God to man: "While we were still sinners, Christ died for the ungodly." Professor Lewis in his *The Four Loves* shows how in human life gift love (agape) and need love (eros) often do coalesce, as when a man, or more often a woman, has the need to love disinterestedly, wanting nothing in return. When perverted this becomes the need to be needed.

Now I will point out that the New Testament has another word for love besides agape, namely *philia*. The nearest we have for it is *friendship*, but that does not convey its full force. We have it in compound terms like 'philosophy', love of wisdom; 'philanthropist', lover of mankind; 'Philadelphia', city of brotherly love. When Christ asks St. Peter three times (John xxi. 15 ff) "Simon, son of Jonas, lovest thou me?" and Peter three times answers "Thou knowest that I love thee," in the first two questions, Jesus uses *agape* for love, but at the third time he uses *philia*. To all three questions Peter replies with *philia*. This suggests that when the Fourth Gospel was written, agape and philia were pretty well synonymous.

So we have four kinds of love, venus, eros, agape and philia. But here are two more: there is affection, *storge* in Greek, and there is *dilectio*, to use a Latin term for love which takes delight in the object for its own excellence rather than for what it means to us; it suggests being *wrapt* in the object's quality; we could call it disinterested *enjoyment*.

In married love, at its best, all these six kinds of love are at work. Venus and eros and affection, of course, at the start. Afterwards there grows a kind of friendship which is aware of the partners sharing a kind of society which is a sort of secret from the outside world, but which must not cut it off. This is part of the meaning of the word 'mate' often used of the spouse. At high moments there is *dilectio* in which one admires and appreciates the other without wanting anything. And finally there is *agape* which is entirely self-giving, thinking only what do I mean to you and not at all what do you mean to me. Both *dilectio* and *agape* are almost impossible to maintain as settled dispositions because of the vanity and egoism of the human soul. But they are called out now and then, *dilectio* in certain blessed times of happiness, and *agape* when one acts purely to please the other and when one has to bridge over a rift from one's own end without waiting for the other. Forgiveness is an act of *agape*; it is needed most in marriage and it is there that it is most difficult. One is more easily hurt by acts of gross injustice, unfair blaming, betrayal of trust, when we have counted on love and the marriage bond to protect us from these things, than we are when injured by outsiders. Forgiveness is also needed when the other imagines an injury which has not been intended.

Even when it is someone not so close to us who has injured us deeply, forgiveness is an agony. Have you ever been hurt to the depth of your soul by the injury

77

of a friend? And then been implored to forgive the injury and take them back into your love and confidence? If you have you will know that no mere 'let bygones by bygones' will do. As Satan says in Milton's *Paradise Lost*: "For never can true reconcilement grow, where wounds of deadly hate have pierced so deep." It costs you a frightful lot to forgive; it smarts. You have, as it were, to bear the injury all over again, and you feel the weight of your friend's guilt. In marriage injuries cut deeper and forgiveness is harder, just because the closeness of the bond and the fact of love make us naked to the shafts of the partner's egoism, blindness and arrogance. There are times in marriage when these things happen, and where forgiving agape is desperately necessary. Most of all perhaps when one's partner is unfaithful and commits adultery. That is a total affront to his or her marriage partner; there where forgiveness is hardest to give it *must* be granted if wanted.

Now, apart from such very painful situations which often do arise, there are less acute but real problems in the living together of man and wife. It is not easy to see a neighbour in those to whom we are linked by nature and by attraction. We tend to assume that the bond of blood or attraction and the deep ties of venereal union, are quite enough to put us in right relations with parent, or spouse, or child. It is perhaps in this kind of tie that we find it hardest to know the other one as a unique person in his or her own right—and not just as father or mother, brother or sister, husband or wife, son or daughter. We slip into thinking that they matter only for their relationships to us. Many a man has never learnt to see his father as a person with his own individuality, and many a marriage has been wrecked because one or both parties have taken it for granted that mutual attraction and a wedding should have solved all the problems of living together. In this matter of love and marriage the man and the woman have each put into it so much emotional capital that the other partner is regarded as an investment of one's own, to pay one dividends. We can be frightfully nice even then; but this is not the same as knowing this man and this woman to whom we are bound by the close bonds of venereal union, of love, marriage and perhaps a family—knowing him or her as one like ourselves, with a meaning of his or her own. Here we have to learn the art of seeing as neighbours those whom God has sent to us through the ties of nature, love and marriage.

Let us recognise it frankly: owing to the vanity of the human soul there is an inherent rivalry between any two human beings in close contact. Each one is dethroned, after outgrowing the romantic love condition where each I is lost in the you. In the new relationship a specific consciousness of I and you emerges. A new orientation is necessary. You may be familiar with Martin Buber's useful exposition of the difference between an 'I and Thou' relationship and the 'I and it' relationship.[4] When I am dealing with an it—whether it be a piece of nature I am studying scientifically, a doll I am playing with, or a piece of steel I am fashioning, I am the only active agent, the only self in operation. I am as it were sovereign in the situation. But when I am confronted with a thou, that thou is another I, looking at me. I am no longer just looking enquiring, mastering, changing, calling the thing in question. I am now being looked at, enquired about and called in question. A botanical specimen does not answer back, but another person can say 'who the devil are you anyway' trying to cope with me. In other words, I am dethroned from a masterly position, and have to adapt myself strategically with another's self to whom I am the object. This is always a prick to one's self-esteem. Children endure it, and soon get cured if they are not alone in the family. But when a man or woman has been idolised in the love dream, he or she can feel very resentful when confronted with another who now is not merely an adoring lover but a self, often calling you in question. Fortunately, that resentment generally comes out in the wash.

But it often goes with a more serious situation. We are all in a bit of a mess inwardly, with our own feelings of inadequacy, our own sensitiveness, our secret unfulfilled hopes. None is a completely harmonious being, and so we tend to regard our neighbour, unconsciously perhaps, as a means of helping us. It is funny, isn't it, how people often fall out without the slightest animosity to one another. It is because we are always trying to solve our own internal problems by expecting something of others. We often do get that help just by the indeliberate influence of the other, especially in marriage. And it's not a question of compatibility, in the usual sense of having the same temperament, interests and tastes. Such a similarity is frequently the field of rivalry, where a real difference of make-up would be better. I have known many happy marriages, but seldom compatible ones, except in the sense of being complementary. I often think that the two patron saints of co-operation are Jack Sprat and his wife.

When I expect my neighbour to give me the esteem, importance or consideration I feel I want, without earning it by my behaviour, then I am using my neighbour to solve my own problems. He or she naturally resents being treated as a means for my satisfaction if I take it as a right. Then I resent his or her resentment, and so antagonism grows. What it comes to is this: in order to be a good neighbour (and in marriage I am neighbour of a special kind to my wife or husband) I must be at unity in myself—and a Christian would add, in order to be at unity within myself I must be at unity with God. When you are a true individual—and individual does not mean separate from others, but undivided within—then you can meet your neighbour without making exorbitant demands upon him or her. What is more, you will have energy to spare, being not merely at the mercy of the other's attitude to you. This does not mean that you will never suffer, or that your partner will never let you down, but the things you endure will not crush you inwardly, make you timid, touchy, irascible, grousy and resentful. All that uses up your inner powers of bridging over the gap from your own end, and makes you wait for the other—and the other waits for you. The result is stalemate and growing resentment.

There are, it seems to me, two main ways in which spouses expect the marriage to make up for some defective state in themselves, and are then disappointed or angry when it does not happen. One is that we bring our own life-style acquired in childhood and in our family constellation, into the marriage. The psychologists have had a good deal to say about this and I will not elaborate it.[5] A spoilt child, seeing himself as the centre of a world which goes out of its way to pamper him, starts marriage with a serious handicap. So does a girl who has had a harsh father, or a boy who hates his mother. Schopenhauer hated his mother; and she was undoubtedly an objectionable woman. He wrote a large part of his philosophic work *The World as Will and Idea*, on the relation of the sexes, with a strong suspicion of women and a deep pessimism about love. But also a girl who dotes on her father, or a boy on his mother, will tend inevitably to compare his wife with his darling mother, and the girl her husband with her beloved father. And so on. If you are looking for a good marriage partner, try to get one who has had a happy but not a spoiled childhood; and do not feel too heroically confident that you will be able to mend a wreck.

The second way in which married people may be oppressive to one another is to expect the partner to compensate for loss of satisfaction in *work* and lack *of ordinary social* contacts. When a man or woman is out of joint with their job, they expect an undue regard for their significance from the partner in marriage. And if they have no real friendship outside and interests, they will be parasitic on the husband or wife and family for recognition and companionship.

Inevitably, I am dealing with skeletons in the marriage cupboard, and that gives a distorted one-sidedness to the picture. But the frequent breakdowns of marriage today seem to call for it. I have been trying to describe the ways in which human egoism and vanity can begin to wreck a marriage. There human egoism and vanity penetrate to the venereal level and often turn the eros relation of love into hate or resentment. Whatever egoism there is in men and women arouses in marriage, to some extent, a sex war. One need not get cynical about this—it has been good-naturedly and jokingly referred to when it has been said the appropriate hymn for a wedding is 'Fight the good fight' or 'He who would valiant be 'gainst all disaster'. The music hall and pantomime make good fun out of it. But there is a serious side to it. It leads to bitterness or a tolerant sense of fatality as when a man will say to other men—"Oh women, we know what they are"; and women to women "Oh! men, they're all alike." Personal resentments turn into sex resentments, and they affect the venereal level itself; copulation becomes an aggressive act and refusal also, in order to show one's power. Again, personal resentments are disguised as disgust at some trivial habit of the other one. Men have left their wives ostensibly because he could not stand her snoring—whereas it is known that where there is no personal grudge the partner's snoring keeps nobody awake. And a woman got a divorce on cruelty because the husband would not give up eating biscuits in bed. One would like to know what was seething underneath. There is always the potentiality of sex warfare; male brutality and female artifice bear witness to a tension between the sexes. There is hardly a married woman who has not sometimes thought her husband clumsy, doctrinaire and brutal; and a married man thought his wife crazy and unscrupulous.

Now this leads us to some of the causes of infidelity to marriage. It is generally believed that a man or a woman going off with someone else is entirely a matter of sensuality—they want a new sexual partner. There is of course something in this. Everybody sighs for new sexual adventures and if we don't follow it up, we get a vicarious pleasure at reading of the sexual scandals in the papers, and about the string of new wives and husbands acquired by film stars and the degenerate peerage.

But in spite of this covetousness for fresh sexual partners, infidelity mostly proceeds from resentment and revenge or some other non-sexual reason. A favourite way for a married man to secure the embraces of another woman is to tell her 'my wife does not understand me'. The probability is that he is understood only too well. The trick works, all the maternal, protective instincts of the second woman are aroused. The personal animosity in the marriage leads to the adultery. I've known cases where the wife is distressed because she says her husband makes excessive sexual demands on her, though she tries to be obliging. Then she makes the mistake of withholding signs of affection in case it should lead to more love making. The truth of that case is that he badly needs signs of affection, and not getting them he tries to secure it in the momentary affection of sexual intercourse. Unmet need for plain simple affection often sends people away to try another man or woman.

Here is another case: when one partner makes the other feel very inferior, either by coming from a better social set or from superior culture and education, the snubbed inferior husband will go to a little insignificant woman from whom he gets admiration, or the snubbed inferior-feeling wife who rightly will not submit to be brought up to his level by being moulded, will seek a love partner who takes her for what she is. That infidelity does not usually spring from thwarted delight in the venereal embrace, is shown by the fact that often the verge of marriage breakdown is accompanied by more frequent and ardent intercourse. It is as if the poor things are trying to find a unity in the blood stream that they cannot get in their meeting as persons. In extreme cases infidelity is the greatest act of vengeance one can take against a partner whom one has come to hate. But enough of this clinical stuff.

Finally, married happiness depends a good deal on man and woman understanding—or at least accepting the difference between male and female love. I mentioned Father D'Arcy's book *The Mind and Heart of Love*. In it he concludes that masculine love is eros and feminine love *agape*—the man demanding and searching, the woman giving and satisfying. I think this is mistaken. Both man and woman can learn to love with *agape*—gift love—and supremely if they know their own personal life as having other resources than those given in the love relation. If they are religious they find their resources in God. Both can show *agape*; it has nothing to do with sex differences at all. Though feminine love can look very like it in its natural devotion, it is really a counterfeit *agape*. The real difference comes in with the fact that the two sexes have a different kind of eros, and therefore also two different kinds of egoism in eros.

Roughly speaking, and to repeat an earlier statement, masculine *eros* is love seeking an object, feminine *eros* is love aroused by an object. You can see this in the way men and women talk. A man will tell his friends why he loves a particular woman and he will tell her. His love is intellectual, he loves her qualities, loves them through her. It is more impersonal than a woman's love. A woman on the other hand loves a man for himself; reasons for loving are for her irrelevant. The objects of a woman's love are more concrete and immediate than a man's. Man on the other hand seeks more universal fields to devote himself to. "The foundations are the province of woman, the superstructure is the man's." A husband will wax enthusiastic about his pet ideas—and is disconcerted to be interrupted with 'what shall I do for supper' or 'do wipe Johnnie's nose'. Conversely, women are often put out by the lack of consideration and attention shown by the male in the hundreds of circumstances in daily life. In such cases, the only safeguard against resentment is to understand

86

the difference, remembering it is possible to be loved just as much as one loves, and even more—but not with the same kind of love.[6]

The two kinds of eros have their own kind of egoism. Man is the romantic, always seeking the ideal woman like Don Juan who was not a sensualist like Casanova, but an incurable idealist. One woman after the other was taken up and dropped, in search of the ideal. The romantic is always liable to neglect the concrete welfare and happiness of the woman he is with—especially the wife. On the other side woman's love, being aroused by and directed to a particular man, is in danger of being possessive and jealous of his dreams and outside concerns.

I think Miss Dorothy L. Sayers was right when she wrote: "The sentiment 'man's love is of man's life a thing apart; 'tis woman's whole existence' is, in fact a piece of male wishful thinking . . . Lovers, husbands, children, households—these are major feminine preoccupations; but not love. It is the male who looks upon amorous adventure as an end in itself, and dignifies it with a metaphysic. The great love lyrics, the great love tragedies, the romantic agony, the religion of beauty, the cult of the *ewig Weibliches* the entire mystique of sex is, in historic fact, of masculine invention . . . Faust and Don Juan, Lovelace and Manfred are not of woman born."[7]

There is one more thing about the different loves in man and woman which M. Thibon points out. Feminine love is much more clear sighted in regard to the object of its affections. It feeds less on illusions. A man's love is a thing of judgments and comparisons; whenever it feels menaced by some lack in the person loved, it has a way of promptly reacting with illusions. Woman on the other hand, can see right through the man she loves without the least detriment to her love itself. The great merit of this—I say it as a male—is that the man has no need to posture and hide his failings and strike important attitudes. By doing so he merely excites her ridicule. In practice, the reciprocity of the two kinds of eros brings about a growing similarity. The love of a wife grows more universal as it comes in contact with her husband's interests; similarly the love of a man shows more practical consideration under the influence of a woman's affection.

There is one great gift granted to the married who have learned each other's kind of love, which can be had in no other love relationship. It is what we may call the gift of divination, of knowing the other one so well that we see their secret longing before they see it themselves. This is what happens: let me put it from the male point of view for brevity's sake—but it must also be reversed. You give the beloved a surprise that is not a complete surprise. You take, or do, or just say something: she says: "How did you know I should be so pleased; I did not know it myself until you gave it me. This is what I wanted, this thing, or act or word, but I did not know I wanted it; I would never have guessed it myself." It requires over half a lifetime to learn this art. The glory of married love depends upon just this power to divine the wishes of the other before they have come into the other's consciousness. Each knows the other better than the other knows himself or herself. Isn't that very near to what we know of God's love for us, 'Who knows our necessities before we ask' and before we know what we want to ask.

6

SEX AND CIVILISATION

WHEN we use the term 'Christianity', we should be careful to see that we may be talking about three different things. We may be referring to a personal faith, or to the institution and life of the Church, or to a culture which has absorbed many Christian outlooks and values without necessarily having Christian belief or church allegiance. In the same way, when we employ the title 'Christian Sex Ethics,' it could mean the standards in sexual behaviour which the Christian believer derives from his personal faith; it could also mean what the Church has codified and expounded on sexual morals; and, in the third place, it could mean the general pattern of ethics (or ideals, if you prefer that misleading word) adopted, but of course not always obeyed, in a civilisation or culture where the predominant religion has been Christianity. A useful examination of the distinction between Christianity as a personal faith and Christianity as an ingredient in a pattern of culture, is to be found in the opening pages of Professor Herbert Butterfield's book *Christianity in European History*,[1] not to be confused with his *Christianity and History*.

I have in these lectures so far been expounding Christian Sex Ethics in terms of conduct derived from personal Christian belief, and tried to show that this belief, formed and fortified by the general Church tradition, does lead to a pattern of sexual conduct which makes for the fulfilment of human living by integrating the biological and erotic with the personal, and these two with the social needs of mankind. This is the approach which most appeals to the modern Western European because he has now come to evaluate everything by the criterion of personal fulfilment and happiness. The aim of personal fulfilment or happiness has come out of our Classical, Christian, Humanist inheritance. Without that inheritance we should not have that aim; it is not natural to the human race. Its roots are in Greek thought, Biblical and Christian religion, and to some extent in Roman politics. It has been nurtured in Western Europe from the eighth century to the fifteenth when the social and emotional life were looked after by institutions, by the idea of law above the will, by the common influence of religious rituals, and by the division of powers in the same culture. European society has been a unique phenomenon, as you may see in modern studies like Karl Jaspers *The Origin and Goal of History*;[2] Wm. Haas *The Destiny of the Mind, East and West*;[3] Christopher Dawson *Christianity and the Rise of European Culture*.[4] It would take too long to unfold the character of what we may call European civilisation. I must confine myself to the dogmatic statement that the significance of the individual grew on top of a certain settlement and unity in the roots of society. At the Renaissance the individual was championed in dissociation from its roots in community, morals and religion. Hence the growth of the power of the modern state to recover the unity. But the state is an association of individuals, not of communities, and it tends to deprive communities of their vitality. But there are some communities which the individualism and the *étatism* and the disintegrating forces of industrial commercialism have not completely extinguished or absorbed. They are the churches, the corporations for learning like our universities, and, for our present interest, above all the family—the family in the sense which Christendom has witnessed and supported. And this family is closely bound up with the sexual mores or customs of our civilisation. The family in modern European society is a smaller and more intimate community than the kin or the class or the tribe. It has been patriarchal in that the father has assumed responsibility for the household and the upbringing of his own children and has not been only the economic breadwinner. The family has been the cultural nursery of the young, who remain with parents long after they could feed themselves in order to imbibe the lore and culture of the civilisation. The wife, though until recently mostly occupied in rearing children and running the home, was an independent person in her own right even when married by family arrangement rather than by her own choice. The quarrels of husbands and wives are quarrels of equals, on the whole. Looking at the history from the point of view of the twentieth-century emphasis on the independence of women, we do not realise the power and freedom accorded to them in this European culture as compared with all others. W. E. H. Lecky who was no friend of the Christian religion insists in his *History of European Morals*,[5] that the principles on which Western Civilisation was founded, were laid by the Christian Church, especially the principles of the sanctity of human life, human brotherhood, the improved status of women and sexual morality, of which he says, "There is probably no other branch of ethics which has been so largely determined by special dogmatic theology."

And then this European family has been a community of persons in the full sense, because of the limitations set by the tradition on sexual experience, namely, a disapproval of pre-nuptial and extra-marital sexual behaviour, and insistence upon lifelong fidelity within marriage. Of course, it has been a turbulent achievement and has had to survive many revolts against it both in practice and theory. But it was there as a norm, and all forms of profligacy were aberrations from it. The question before the twentieth century in the modern West is whether we can preserve the positive achievements of our European culture, if the sexual discipline it enjoined is seriously slackened, as it appears to be in our own time in England.

I am not defending the Christian ethical standard because it is part of this civilisation. A Christian will not put down the survival of any civilisation as an absolute good to which all human behaviour should be subservient. There are times when the Christian community has to resist or withdraw from the civilisation it co-exists with. For a Christian's ultimate citizenship is in Heaven not on Earth. But I am concerned to say two things. The first is this: those critics who hold that Christian sex ethics have been over-rigorous, and think that society and individuals would be better and happier with a freer sexual code, are in serious error if they believe it possible to abandon the sexual discipline and retain all the other characteristics of European civilisation. The modern hedonist who considers the immediate happiness of the individual to be the sole criterion of conduct and who says he doesn't care about civilisation, has a strong position; but he is a sociological idiot if he believes that mankind can abandon moral effort, refuse any suppression and relinquish every inner *ascesis*, and still count on the continuance of cultural achievement.

The second thing I would say about the idea of being indifferent to the fate of civilisation, is that it would be all right for those who have the makings of a saint and a martyr in them, and the heroic stamina to live by the call of the spirit however contrary to the trend of his culture that call may be. But if he is an ordinary but honest human being he will admit that he is very much dependent on the direction of his society and its culture through large patches of his life when the superhuman powers of the spirit are not at their full stretch. If there is a collapse of a culture with nothing outside the individual's intention and will to back it up then the only survivals will be the unscrupulous villain and the completely detached saint.

I am asking you to assume without proof that a disintegration of sexual morals will affect deleteriously all the other ingredients of our civilisation: its emphasis on the significance of persons, its rule of law against arbitrary power, its disinterested science, its literature and art, even its reasons for rebellion, for rebellion has to have a norm to withstand. Modern young people have largely lost the experience of disobedience because nobody gives them orders, except the state.

I am also asking you to believe that when I talk about European culture, I do not mean the disintegrated form of it which marks the nineteenth and twentieth centuries. In this very recent period some end-products of the culture have been cut away from their social, religious and intellectual roots. So we have its secularism, its economic values regarded as supreme, its arrogant destruction of the bases of life in the earth, in community and in religion which gives man resources from outside civilisation itself. As a result much of what has been creative in Western society has been and is being destroyed. I am not asking that this parasitic fungus on a great culture should be saved by a tightening up of sexual behaviour. Rather, I am arguing that if there is to be any creative renewal from the ground up, it will only come from groups of people living in this period who are involved responsibly in it, but who are not of it—and who have discovered that if the personal and family and love life is to be the cradle of the forces of renewal, then the personal and family and love life will have to be what was the norm in the flowering of European civilisation.

Of course, the observance of Christian sex ethics inevitably creates a strain which is creative as well as painful, because ethics as well as culture involves a continual battle with impulse and inclination. Sigmund Freud, the founder of psycho-analysis, realised this, though he did not much want to admit it. He had been so successful in tracing the neuroses of modern *bourgeois* Europeans to sexual repressions, that he tried to believe this repression could account for the universal human condition, from the Oedipus situation in Greek legend, even from the totemism of primitive tribes — to the latest patient of his own. But Freud could not help knowing that without some suppression of sexual impulse there is no civilisation. In its earlier phase Freud's theory taught that guilt for the sexual sin of incest was the cause of social organisation and culture. Then after more acquaintance with simple peoples it became obvious that if there is no social and cultural rule to transgress there can be no feeling of guilt. Anyhow, Freud seems to have been all the time worried by the fact that civilisation requires restriction of sexual opportunity; his clinical experience in twentieth-century Central Europe taught him how these sexual restrictions produce psychic conflicts and neuroses. He could not dismiss civilisation as a disaster yet he could not but regard it as a misfortune. Hence the hesitancy and honest doubt in one of his later works, *Civilization and its Discontents*.[6] I think the trouble was that Freud derived his view of man from the restricted experience of the highly self-conscious twentieth-century European in a culture where there was no longer any integration between men's conscious aims and the emotional, biological and community foundation of life. In such a period sex is not a natural passion which needs curbing for cultural purposes; sex becomes 'a problem' intellectually, and it becomes the field of experience which draws to itself all the frustrated cravings of the inner life. The European men and women of today tend to feel that all their unsatisfied longings must be due to frustrated sexuality. Of this I will speak further in the last lecture.

Freud was an honest thinker. He would rather remain perplexed than be recklessly confident. In this he contrasts favourably with many who have attacked the traditional sex ethics of Christendom, attacked it at least by implication. You have Dr. R. Briffault in his large work *The Mothers* who writes of "The moral standards as applied to sexual relations and the radical product of that exaltation of ritual purity which pronounced a curse upon sex, stigmatised women as the instrument of Satan and poured scorn upon motherhood." This would be an apt description of the attitude which tried to invade Christendom through sects of Mithraic and Manichaean origin and gave rise to the powerful movement of the Cathari described by Sir Stephen Runciman in *The Mediaeval Manichee*.[7] It is true that many early churchmen were carried away by these attitudes, but in general they were condemned by the Church as heresies. It is not the case that heretical movements always have liberalising tendencies. Here is a case where the unorthodox sectaries were extreme rigorists and the orthodox more liberal and balanced.

Dr. Briffault has a recent disciple in Mr. Gordon Rattray Taylor who in his book *Sex in History*[8] evinces dislike of the patriarchal family, associated as it has been with a high doctrine of sexual continence outside marriage, and he sighs for a return of what he calls a 'matrist' form of society where sexual relations are much more free. Mr. Havelock Ellis also wanted the strict code of sexual ethics relaxed—and any who look at his enormous output, especially *Studies in the Psychology of Sex*, should also read the biography of him by Arthur Calder Marshall, where the tragic fact emerges that this life long concern for sexual freedom was a compensation for his own incapacity for full sexual love. The earlier Bertrand Russell, in *Marriage and Morals* advocated a complete separation of the three aspects of the sexual relation in man and woman, namely venereal union, love and marriage, each of these to be sought with a different partner. He did not, however, go so far as Demosthenes in ancient Greece who said bluntly "We have wives for child-bearing, *hetairae* for companionship and slaves for lust."

All this sort of writer, with the exception of Freud, seem to ignore the possibility that a relaxation of the sexual code, if it becomes general, will inevitably mean a destruction of the civilisation they otherwise seem to value. So I have now to introduce you to a solid body of sociological material which supports my statement of a close connection between the growth of a culture and civilisation and the restriction of sexual opportunity within certain limits. I have in an earlier lecture mentioned the view of the Russian philosopher Berdyaev that the clamping down of sexual and emotional forces by asceticism in early and mediaeval

Christendom, was a conquest over nature within man. This power over nature was projected outward in forming the political and cultural pattern of European society, and at the Renaissance it began to master physical nature itself by applied science and technique. In his book *The Meaning of History*, Berdyaev develops this theme.[9] Christianity means the death of the great God Pan; it rescued man from his immersion in elemental nature, it set him free from submission to the natural world by establishing his roots in the eternal world. "When immersed in nature and communing with its inner life, man could neither apprehend it scientifically nor master it technically," and I would add myself, could not either transcend tribal culture or make associations on the European model. "The result of man's Christian liberation from nature was when he discovered an inner spiritual world, when he undertook a tremendous heroic struggle against the natural elements in order to overcome his subjection to nature, and to forge an image of himself as a free human personality." This is also my conclusion; for things do not happen in history by a process of inevitable social evolution, as if all men had it inherent in them to become what we Europeans have become, or as if all peoples would even want to be like us if they had a good look at what we are. No, we are what we are because men started something somewhere — and if they had not we would not be what we are. Therefore I say that European man's achievement in politics, law, art, science and in promoting the significance of the individual, have their origin in early western man's

99

battles with nature in himself. The modern scientific laboratory is the cultural descendent of the hermitage and the monastery.

Part of that mastery over nature in man's own life has been a mastery over the sexual impulse, to a degree in European Christendom not known elsewhere. But it has been known or practised to some degree throughout mankind's civilised history. All cultural development has meant a limitation of sexual drives. B. Malinowski, in his *Sex and Repression in Savage Society* shows that even an elementary culture demands some limit on sexual adventure. He was followed up by the researches of Mr. J. D. Unwin published in 1934 by the Oxford University Press under the title *Sex and Culture*.[10] His conclusion, reached after a review of many societies and civilisations, is that when social regulations forbid indiscriminate satisfaction of the sexual impulses, the emotional conflict is expressed in another way, and that what we call civilisation has been built up by sacrifices in the gratification of innate desires. "A greater or lesser mental development has accompanied a limitation or extension of sexual opportunity." Unwin correlates three types of religion with three kinds of society described by their sexual regulations. "Societies that permitted pre-nuptial freedom were in the *zoistic* condition and produced little culture beyond tribal survival. Societies that imposed an irregular or occasional continence were in the *manistic* condition: these have a more elaborate social system. Societies that enforced complete pre-nuptial continence were in the *deistic* condition, and these have the maximum of intellectual and creative energy. He deduces that the greatest social energy and impulse for civilisation-building is a correlate of the strictest of sexual patterns, namely that of absolute monogamy and extra-marital continence.

There is ample evidence that societies with the strictest sexual codes have been of the patriarchal type. Christianity did not inaugurate the patriarchal family; that was the pattern of all the great civilisations of antiquity. The name 'Patriarchal Family' now suggests to many that wife and children were oppressed chattels of a dominating husband and father, and for many people today it recalls the jealous property holding clan of the Victorian age with no rights and liberties for any member but the male head—pictured in Galsworthy's *Forsyte Saga*. There are as many accounts in literature of the dominating and possessive mother, even in our nominally patriarchal culture. Others, when they hear of 'the patriarchal family' picture warlike males in older cultures raiding the land of their neighbours and carrying off their women, and then keeping them in seclusion from the possible attention of other males. Here let me interject two anecdotes. Dr. R. R. Marett, formerly Rector of Exeter, and before that founder of the department of Anthropology here in Oxford, and from whom I learned some anthropology, used to say in his playful way after describing savage marriage customs, "Of course, women were never really married by capture; they always pretended they were, as they do still." The other story is about the traveller in Africa who came across a native woman turning over the ground with a digging stick, and near by was her husband sitting playing on a flute. The European traveller came back and wrote a book, in which he said: "Here is a plain case of the oppression of women. The man has told the woman to work and she has meekly obeyed." A reviewer of the book quite rightly declared "that this is hopelessly naïve. If the author had known anything about the real world, he would have seen that the actual situation was this: the woman had told the man to work, and he hadn't obeyed."

What then is the character of the patriarchal family, which has the strictest sexual moral code, and which underlies the European family of Christendom? I will give it you in the words of a Professor of Clinical Psychology at Columbia University, New York, Abram Kardiner. You will find it in his book *Sex and Morality*.[11] He is not obviously a Christian believer, and he proves that the traditional and rigorous sex morality has its price in mental and personal strains for those who have not come to terms with it squarely and whole-heartedly. Nevertheless, this is what he says in a chapter entitled "The good effects of sex morality": "We do not know of any great civilisation that has had a polyandrous pattern; we do know of some that had a polygamous pattern. But none of them compares with those cultures that have had a monogamous pattern. Those cultures that have endured longest and made the greatest contributions to what we call civilisation have been monogamous and patriarchally orientated." This has nothing to do with a dominating father. Kardiner goes on to show that the patriarchal family has these effects because that kind of family combines maternal care of the young with the responsibility of the father for the cultural training of the offspring, and brings father and child in close personal relations. To quote again "There is the close and constant proximity of parent and child, which is more favourable to the development of strong emotional attachments. The constant attendance of the mother aids the child in his struggle for existence before his own resources are developed . . . What is of highest importance is the persistent care of the child by *both* mother and father . . . The presence of the one father is very important. His attention is concentrated on his one mate and on their offspring . . . The important thing about these roles of mother and father is that they are constant and persistent. It is apparent from comparative studies of cultures with different family patterns that the human infant flourishes best with one effective parent of each sex. A child who is given persistent and affectionate care gains a certain naïve conception of himself as a powerful and self-sufficient creature and of the outer world as a source of interest and pleasure. When his care is poor the reverse is true. The world becomes a place full of disagreeable things from which the child withdraws." Thus for Professor Kardiner. I have myself known children, promising and confident, lose their nerve and tend to become failures when a marriage breaks up and one parent departs; this curiously affects the boy most when his father leaves. The emotional insecurity that ensues turns a confident child into an anxiety case.

The main contention in Kardiner's diagnosis is that

because of the security and assurance which the child of a monogamous and patriarchal family enjoys, the young of the European family have shown an enterprise and constructive social power not reached elsewhere.

Of course, the patriarchal family requires of its members a good deal of renunciation. The wife must be chaste and devoted to the family, the children must be taught to obey and to endure discipline; the husband takes on much personal responsibility beyond merely providing the physical needs of the household. The family under these conditions has added many functions to its basic sexual and reproductive ones. That is why the patriarchal family pattern has been such a great force in the development of western culture.

All the great world civilisations in Europe and Asia have had a patriarchal structure in the family. In this they differed from the matrist societies which preceded them. The decline of the classical civilisation of the ancient Mediterranean world was partly marked by the break-up of the patriarchal family which had been the vehicle of continuity amid social and military upheavals. In the latter days of the Graeco-Roman culture men cared more for outside pleasures and public life, and satisfied sexual impulses with other men, or with slaves and prostitutes. The patriarchal family reappeared again in western Christendom, though in some respects it had a character different from that of the ancient world, except Confucian China. In both China and Europe the patriarchal family was a feature of the whole of society, and was not confined to an upper and ruling class. This kind of family also ensured the mature and equal sexual obligations between husband and wife who belonged to each other exclusively. In spite of many movements and ideas running counter to this new kind of patriarchal family, it persisted strongly until weakened by the socially disintegrating influence of the industrial revolution which tended to subordinate natural community bonds to the pursuit of wealth. After a short-lived alliance between puritan morals and economic enterprise which kept the family pattern with a certain artificial rigidity and some hypocrisy, the decay of those morals left no banks to stem the flood which substituted economic and state relations for domestic local and neighbourhood unities. Yes, the family in an eviscerated form has survived, but the household is no longer the primary place of social and cultural activity; at its worst it is but the shelter and kitchen for a number of independent wage earners; and in reaction to this, a kindergarten of pampered and harassed children. That is of course the seamy side; there is another side.

It is one of the strongest grounds of modest confidence that today the family has not been quite abolished by the weakening effects of sexual licence and the high divorce figures. A recent writer says: "In England, family is all pervasive: duty is done to the kindred and obligations extracted from them everywhere, especially when there is capital. The family must be provided for at someone's expense; competition must yield to its demands."[12] Yes true, but what if the spring has gone out of it; mere welfare and economic alleviation will not save it. True, people are still clinging to the family pattern, though in the situation its brittleness is the cause of much anxiety and loss of nerve. To that we shall turn in the next and last lecture which will be devoted to an examination of the forces in our society which threaten the institution of marriage and the Christian sex ethics which go with it—or in other words what is today making the observance of that ethic more difficult and leading to an obsession with sex.

7

THE EROTIC OBSESSION OF THE TWENTIETH CENTURY

In this last lecture of the course on Christian Sex Ethics, I propose to enquire what is the character of twentieth-century society, especially in the Anglo-Saxon world; and how that character makes the observance of Christian standards difficult, difficult in a new sense. That observance has always been difficult, in the sense that the powerful elemental forces of sex have time and again pressed against the limitations upon their expression, which civilisation in general and Christian culture in particular have imposed. Whenever a strong impulse is denied indiscriminate outlets, then unless the controlling forces engage as much or more emotional energy than the impulse itself, the mind will turn to the thwarted impulse, and the impulse will acquire a measure of importance out of all proportion to its natural place in life.

European History has thus had several periods in which the sexual basis of life has had obsessive attention, precisely because it is in this culture that the vital and emotional forces have been most rigorously controlled in the interests of civilisation and ethics. This control was possible because the underlying controlling influence was religious, for the Christian

107

religion unlike humanist ethics does not confront elemental instinct and passion with purely rational and social demands. The Christian religion took hold of the mind of European man at a level below and behind his biological and emotional life. It has been the greatest error of the rational humanism of the last three centuries to believe that reason could master the passions, even reason in the service of civilisation. The fact is that only when the passions are looked after, directed and catered for, by the deep, mysterious and worshipful forces of religious faith and ritual, can the top-storey of human life be free to master itself by rational purpose and enquiry. Reason is the clearest part of the mind, and in order to function freely it requires underneath it a certain order in the passions and emotions. If there is chaos underneath, the rational and civilising powers will be unable to master the chaos, but they will be trying to do so, like the tongue touching the aching tooth for an imagined sense of relief.

This sort of diagnosis helps, I think, to account for what I have called the erotic obsession of the twentieth century. It is a highly intellectual obsession, with a blind unconscious underside to it. The intellectual obsession is revealed in the amount of talk, discussion, serious writing and magazine advice, novels and monographs on the sexual problem. The unconscious underside is revealed by the impulse for wider and more indiscriminate sexual experimentation, in plain fornication and adultery, in repeated attempts to secure satisfaction by changes in marriage partners. And it is all taken very solemnly. That is what makes the twentieth-century obsession different in kind from preceding ones.

We know of the tortured preoccupation with sex in the waning period of Graeco-Roman civilisation. The sensual hedonism of that age should not be regarded merely as a lapse into sensational pleasure-seeking; it should also be estimated as an outstanding example of the way the soul of man reverts to the pulse of the blood stream, with, of course, sophisticated allurements, when a declining culture no longer holds the emotional loyalty of its adherents. It is an aspect of the perennial tendency to seek, blindly or consciously, on a more elemental level, either in the stream of nature or in the hidden forces of the soul, a compensation or cure for breakdowns in the more artificial creations of art, science, politics and culture. As we see in politics, all radical revolutions have looked for a principle of healing in an attempted recovery of the untutored and undistorted state of nature. That is why the influence of Rousseau was much greater than that of all the clever rationalists of the Enlightenment. This represents a reversion to nature on the conscious plane. On a wholly indeliberate level the non-seeing but strongly-feeling unconscious part of the soul gropes for immersion in the pulsating life stream; and sex is the most direct avenue for that. Abandonment to venereal experiences, however, by this kind of reaction on the part of civilised peoples is never a return to simple naïve and innocent sexuality. It is dressed up sophistically, and you get all kinds of sexual perversions; the more outrageous they are, the more sex is turned to from frustrations in other parts of life.

I said that the declining centuries of Graeco-Roman culture produced this kind of obsession with sex; it was a sort of reversion to sensuality from over-sophistication. At the same time, in the early centuries of Christendom, there was another kind of obsession due to the resistance of the instincts to the severe damping down of natural forces by the powers of the spirit in mastering nature within man. A similar kind of obsession took hold of people in the later Middle Ages, with the breakup of the earlier mediaeval synthesis of reason, ethics and passion.[1] In the eighteenth century there was what has been called the 'Erotic Obsession of the Age of Reason', where the colossal power of sex breaks through and tries to capture the dry and sterile works of reason. This erotic reaction produced a great mythology nourished by the ebullition of flesh and blood, and there was a survival of it in the nineteenth century, as can be seen in such works as Mario Praz *The Flesh, Death and the Devil in Nineteenth Century Romanticism*.

Now the twentieth-century situation seems quite different. In the earlier periods of sexual obsession a lot of its force lay just in the fact that sexual enjoyment is fun and gains a zest from the prohibitions of its indiscriminate exercise by a tradition of custom and morals. Departures from the tradition were dashing daring and naughty escapades. Now, this is no longer so. Venereal experiences outside the bounds of marriage are either casual or invested with a solemn prophylactic significance, on the ground that suppression produces mental disease. But the apparent casualness in extra-marital sex experience can be deceptive. It can conceal fantasies of vanity and what the psychologists call ego reinforcement. We have read in the press that, in some places, the loss of virginity in schoolgirls is registered by a badge; it becomes a symbol of emancipation and status.

It is not easy to understand the twentieth-century situation. It seems to me to be marked by an obsession with sex for non-sexual reasons; and the resort to indiscriminate sexual experience does not appear to be a great source of joy and freedom. It is rather like the attitude of a man who said to me in a bus queue, "I'm fed up with the pictures, but I keep on going." It is as if some satisfactions are sought in greater sexual licence, by a kind of inner compulsion which becomes more insistent the smaller the emotional reward it brings. I interpret this greater resort to sexual licence as an example of a general law that when men and women suffer from frustrations in other spheres of life, then frustrations are focused upon the sexual sphere, and it is felt that there the secret of freedom and fulfilment is to be found. We must remember, however, that talk about sex does to some extent provide much of the releasing influence that actual behaviour is supposed to give. That is why it is not safe to deduce actual conduct from the talk about it. This is especially true in sexual matters. Professor Crane Brinton in his *A History of Western Morals*, quite rightly says: "It may be true that Homo Sapiens spends more time and energy fantasying, thinking, talking and writing about sex than in doing anything about it. In the frank

language of our era—or, at any rate of our novels—
there is a great deal of paper tail in the world. One
doubts whether Don Juan actually possessed those
famous 1,003 Spanish ladies. In the West generally,
and especially after the introduction of Christian
prohibitions added zest to fornication, men and
women have found in sexual conquests a great reinforcement of their egos. Moreover, from the very fact that
love-making is almost always conducted in privacy, it
is easy indeed to claim a conquest never in fact achieved
. . . Do not therefore conclude that because there is a
change in the way men talk and write about sexual
matters there is a corresponding change in their
conduct."[2]

I agree with that, but however unreliable it may be to
infer what is done from what is talked about, the fact
that much is said in order to be believed, whether done
or not, is a sign of what I am trying to establish: that
sexual laxity today, whether in act or in mind, is something to which people turn as a compensation for
disappointments in other directions. Before developing
this thesis, I should say I am not ignoring the plain
truth, often repeated, that this laxity is due to a loss of
moral standards as transmitted by families from one
generation to another, and that the upholding of these
standards derived most of its force from close association with the Christian tradition. But I am impressed
by the fact, obvious to me in the earlier part of this
century, that the traditional standards of sexual morals
derived from Christendom informed several generations
of people who had severed all connection with the life

and thought of the Christian Church. If this humanist sexual morality, built into the succession of generations, had kept its hold, we should not have the present obsession with sex as the sphere of deliverance from inhuman restraints.

There is one big and curious feature of the present situation to be noticed. There is no sign that laxity in fornication and adultery is competing with marriage. People do not avoid marriage and commit fornication instead. Along with the tendency towards promiscuity, affecting now the very young, there goes a younger marriage age, great store set on matrimony, desire for a home of one's own, men spending more of their time and money on it; women working to enrich it, and the spoiling of children. All this hints at some hidden connection between the drive for more sexual opportunities and a hankering after domestic bliss as a shelter from the aridity and fearfulness in the larger world. While the family as an institution to be believed in is disappearing, as a repository of emotional smugness it is sought after desperately, though without much sense of commitment. And this family, held together for purely individual needs, without much loyalty to it as an institution, seems unable to bear the weight of meeting all the psychic needs which wider communities used to cater for. I guess this may be a big element in sex satisfaction hunting outside marriage. It may seem unintelligible of me to suggest that craving for family life and craving for sexual satisfactions outside marriage have the same root. But this is so, because the family as a unit and the biological life stream to which eros reverts, are both on the same side of the line which separates the organic and living from the artificial, rational and technical sides of society. The family is still a natural co-operative unit, in spite of its invasion by the utilitarian and competitive and standardising characteristics of our society; and sexual experience in comparison with the rackets of our civilisation is an elemental union of bodies with at least a momentary touch of affection.

Nevertheless, just because the modern family fails to be a repository of emotional security, young people try to get below the commercial and restive and rivalrous relations with which this civilisation surrounds them, and without reasoning it out they turn to the sexual level for a substitute.

Here is a striking account of the attitude of the young in a responsible report on *The Youth Service in England and Wales*, 'The Albemarle Report'.[3]

"In more homes than formerly, the mother goes out to work as well as the father; and this has deprived some adolescents of the necessary feeling of assurance that, even though they may wish to be in it only 'to eat and sleep', the home *is there* as a warm entity . . . Even the strong interest of many parents in television, which often causes them to have the set switched on for almost the whole of each evening, has probably taken from some adolescents the sense that their parents are ready and willing to listen to their stories of the day, or to discuss a new outfit, or simply that they are there, in spirit as well as in fact, to be turned to as occasion wills . . . In spite of all this we do not think the assumption that married life is right and desirable has yet been generally undermined . . . Meanwhile much of the outside world constantly tries to persuade them to believe this or think that, to try this or laugh at that. Yet the realities of their daily work, the small sense of status this gives them, often makes them feel (whatever the friendly public voices say) that at the bottom the outside world regards them as indistinguishable units, a mass. What wonder that they often react into a defensive refusal to give of their inner selves. 'It's all brainwashing,' they say fiercely, equally of those who would 'sell' them soap, records, drink, politics, religion, 'the whole lot are out to brainwash you'. 'Why should I buy it?' Yet the fierceness with which they can say this indicates an acute disappointment . . . When something attracts their loyalty and seems not to be a 'sell', they will show and accept leadership and discipline of a high order."

I think the two important points in that statement are these. First, that the vehemence of the protest against being sold something, indicates an acute disappointment. Secondly, that religion and politics—and presumably ethics and character building—tend to be put down to the same rackets as induce the business world to create more and more wants in people.

This illustrates the first of three main reasons I would advance for the sexual obsession of the twentieth century. People unknowingly are driven to venereal experience, and hope for a great sense of fulfilment in it, as a refuge from or compensation for a sense of deprivation elsewhere. The crudest form of this is just a resort to sexual activity as a kind of narcotic, as one might turn to drink or opium. And sex is an even more cogent relief from the pain of individuality and its problems. It is a commonplace that sexual desires arise not always from natural passion for union with one of the opposite sex, but from a demand to escape from anxiety, however temporarily. Economic anxieties, worries about esteem and status, intolerable personal relations, hating one's work or despising it, general feelings of failure or cowardice —all this sort of anxiety can be momentarily shed in the sexual embrace. There is plenty of evidence that in economic depressions there was a turning to sex and fornication on a frantic scale, by men in responsible positions whose economic position was threatened.[4] And it must be added that economic anxiety plays the same kind of irritant role in a prosperous and welfare society where wealth advancement and class improvement is a perpetual urge. I conclude therefore that the kind of maniacal consciousness of sex today and the incessant chase after sexual satisfaction do not represent an overpowering rise of primitive passion or an idyllic reverence for sex, but are rather a symptom of underlying anxiety about life, or ego-insecurity as it is called. In a Pelican book *Sex and the Social Order*, Georgina H. Seward, puts it this way: "People in our competitive individualised society have an exorbitant need for affection and reassurance. It is this need for human response rather than a genuine sexual desire which leads them into the tense, clutching types of relationship so prevalent among us. Sexual possession of another somehow assures an individual and bulwarks his ego defences, taking the place of a partnership based on mutual love."

It is not therefore, I contend, that a wave of sexual sensuality has weakened marriage. It is much more likely that the insecurity of marriage and the loss of full personal affection in the family engenders the emotional insecurity. And this emotional insecurity makes for a turning to sexual union at almost any price. Many factors contribute to the instability of the family. One is that owing to the destruction of real communities outside the family, such as those created by work associations for good work, neighbourhood togetherness, bonds of profession, creed—owing to a weakening of all communities which arouse emotional attachment, an enormous emotional capital is locked up in marriage. Today, as in the Victorian era, "family or home life may best be appraised by the store men set upon it for affection they miss in other areas of their lives". This is quoted from an important book: *The Political Community, A Study of Anomie*.[5] The author adds: "The average young American, if asked his aim in life, may reply . . . that he wants something resembling the stereotyped ivy-covered cottage with a pretty and ever-loving wife, two 'kids' and a car." If marriage and the family is the only refuge from utilitarian and rat-race pursuits, then emotional demands are made upon the partners by each other which are exorbitant, and disappointment is bound to ensue; estrangement and resentment easily follow.

Then there is the insecurity of the family in a society where divorce is an open possibility. When divorce was an exceptional legal option for exceptionally hard cases, and lifelong monogamy still the norm, little harm was done. Where the possibility of divorce is taken for granted everywhere, even the monogamous marriage loses its character as an element of stability. "Even the non-divorcing married couple is faced with a persistent burden of insecurity and anxiety," writes Dr. J. V. L. Casserley.[6] He continues "Even after a marriage has been contracted, the very awareness that the divorcing expedient exists makes it possible to magnify and dwell upon differences and frictions which in a healthier state of society would be laughed at and forgotten." The same kind of warning has been given by Professor Kardiner.[7] Margaret Mead describes the emotional strain in a divorcing society where husbands and wives nevertheless hope they can maintain their marriage. When divorce is a fairly open door, enormous care to satisfy the other partner and not to arouse his or her suspicions, is required. An emotional clutchingness which is very wearing, "an endless incitement to anxious effort," has to do duty for what in former generations was performed by the unshakeable conviction that marriage was permanent. "It was safe to be romantic when there was no real danger that new romances could tempt you away."[8]

All this is support for my first consideration that it is largely marriage and family insecurity that sends people to sex exploits in general—and to search for emotional satisfaction in perhaps other partnerships.

My second consideration is the large extent to which sexual adventure, especially when it is disapproved, reinforces a weak sense of one's own significance. I pointed out that in marriage one is dethroned from a position of superiority and has to live together with husband and wife as equals—all defences and disguises are down; all masks stripped off. To anyone with a painful feeling of inner poverty in himself or herself this is a great trial. And when men are given little significance in monotonous work, are easily replaceable and have no sense of responsible citizenship or powers of skill, then they expect tributes to their significance beyond what they earn as a human being. Not getting it in the family, as indeed they should not, sexual irregularity is a great temptation. And women who have worked before marriage and lived in a greater world often find that marriage and motherhood is a narrow and boring vocation; again infidelity offers a thrilling outlet.

All along, of course, prohibitions of indiscriminate sexual behaviour have added a piquant attraction to breaking of the rules, and this is a powerful reinforcement of a weak ego. That is why fornication has now become a field for the expression of rivalry, prowess, record-making and convention breaking and the distinction of being a highly individual 'outsider'. Sexual conquest out of bounds is possibly the easiest way to ego reinforcement, and when there is a diminishing area for other forms of contest, in work, sport, political argument, civil loyalties, national spirit—and when recreations become more solitary like newspaper reading, the cinema, wireless and television (solitary, however gregariously engaged in)—then sexual adventure will grow in extent along with violence and destructiveness in a culture where people cannot feel themselves real persons unless they become notorious.

I cannot delineate more fully here the ways in which modern society which has set such store on individuality and encouraged its development, has in its second industrial revolution and its public life narrowed the fields in which individuality can express itself. In such a society sex is the one field where individual aberration can be pursued. But it is a self-defeating pursuit, because the outrageousness of a practice diminishes with its prevalence, and soon ceases to be a sensation for bolstering up a poverty stricken personality.

The third consideration I would advance must be stated very briefly. It is covered by a good deal of what I have already said. Sexual adventure outside the bonds of marriage is sought after, mostly quite unconsciously, as a counterweight to the rackets of modern life. Quite apart from getting and keeping a job, even the school and university are realms of pressure and demand rather than of support and security; so is the status-raising family constellation. There is no home for the soul. However much egoism and emulation enter into sexual adventure, sexual intercourse does penetrate to the biological and pre-conscious level, and even when least enriched by personal affection, it provides moments of intimacy and tenderness. Extra-marital sex experience is undoubtedly sought after in many cases because of poverty of affection and esteem in family, marriage and society. I think the present wave of sex licence is in large measure a reaction to uprootedness from nature, local attachments, social feeling and affection. This has been accentuated by women entering into the get-ahead and competitive status activities. Both halves of the human species are now in the rat race.

Sex is the quickest way from the harsh realities of a mainly economic civilisation to the realm of Nature and of mystery. It is a terrible reflection on our go-ahead culture that the one place of warmth and intimacy left is flesh.

This last lecture has been one of large generalisation and much speculation of my own. It therefore carries no authority. But however inept, it has I hope helped you to realise that the modern sex problem is not entirely the making of individuals, but that they are largely the products of an inhuman culture—one in which the scales are heavily loaded against individuals trying to live by the standards of Christian sex ethics. It is not so much moral degeneration as cultural dis-integration that lies at the bottom of twentieth-century erotic obsession.

I conclude with this observation. The practice of Christian sex ethics is not to be recovered by preaching the ethics. If what I have tried to convey has any cogency, a renewed, creative and fully personal ful-filment of sexuality will only come from people who are aware of the pressure of a debilitated civilisation, and without contracting out of it, can put down their roots in an alternative culture. Christianity is such a culture. Its moral demands are not its main contribution. Underneath those demands is a whole way of life, of deep emotional power bringing its believers in touch with the ultimate mystery of existence, more permanent than the ups and downs of histories and culture. Religion and sex have been closely linked in the history of the human race. That is the ground upon which I assert that religion provides the kind of security and resources which men and women are now vainly seeking by an exaltation of sex in order to counterbalance the impoverishing influence of an over-sophisticated culture. You can only really live in the world fruitfully, happily and co-operatively if you have resources not given by the world. You can only appreciate fruitfully the good things of the world — and sexual love is one of the greatest — if you don't trust them overmuch or seek salvation in them.

I

1 Bertrand Russell: *Marriage and Morals* (London, 1955 edition), p. 43.
2 For the theory of polarity, see R. W. Emerson's essay on *Compensation*; Geoffrey Sainsbury: *The Theory of Polarity* (London, 1927); Lawrence Hyde: *An Introduction to Organic Philosophy*. An essay on the Reconciliation of the Masculine and Feminine Principles (London, 1955). For male and female cosmic powers, see A. Bertholet: *Das Geschlecht der Gottheit* (Tübingen, 1934).
3 Nicholas Berdyaev: *The Meaning of the Creative Act* (New York, 1955) Chapters ii and viii. *Slavery and Freedom* (New York, 1943) Part I, Chapter 3; Part II, Chapter 4.
   cf. E. Lampert: *The Divine Realm* (London, 1944), pp. 92 ff.
4 Martin Buber: *Moses* (New York, 1946), p. 50.
5 Mother Julian of Norwich: *Revelations of Divine Love*. Chapters 58 to 63.
6 Karl Barth: *Kirchliche Dogmatik*, iii. the section on *the Work of Creation* and the section on *Freedom in Community* (Eng. Tr., Church Dogmatic. New York, 1936 ff.).
7 Martin Buber: *Good and Evil* (Eng. Tr., New York,

1952) Part I.

8 Ephesians v. 22, 23.

9 London. Printed for Richard Bishop. 1642.

10 Origen: *De Principiis*. ii. 6 (Eng. Tr., London, 1936), p. 111.

11 *De Trinitate*. Book xii. Chapters 5 to 7.

12 Simone de Beauvoir: *The Second Sex* (Eng. Tr. New York, 1955), p. 636.

13 Roy Campbell's translation: Penguin Classics.

14 Translated by E. Allison Peers (London, 1946).

15 St. Bernard: *Sermones in Cantica*, lxxxiii.

2

1 In *Christian Behaviour*, 1943. Republished in *Mere Christianity* (Fontana Books), p. 87.

2 London, 1960.

3 See e.g. B. K. Malinowski: *Sex and Repression in Savage Society* (London, 1927); Margaret Mead: *Male and Female* (London, 1950).

4 op. cit., pp. 253-4.

5 London, 1959.

6 *The Bent World*, Chapter on 'The Divorcing Society' (Oxford, 1955).

7 op. cit., p. 186.

3

1 New York, 1960.

2 *The Symposium*, XXIII.

3 *The Meaning of Love* (Eng. Tr., London, 1945).

4 *The Four Loves* (New York, 1960), pp. 124 ff.

5 New York, 1936.

6 Eng. Tr., London, 2nd Ed. 1951.

7 New York, 1955.

8 Eng. Tr., *Love in the Western World* (New York, 1956).

9 In *Essays presented to Charles Williams* (Oxford, 1947).

10 Introduction to Miss Sayers' translation of Dante's *The Divine Comedy*, II, *Purgatory* (Penguin Classics), p. 43.

11 *The Mothers* (London, 1927).

12 *On the Nature of Things*, Book IV.

13 R. M. MacIver, *Society* (New York, 1937), p. 211.

14 Ralph Linton, *The Study of Man* (New York, 1936), p. 175.

15 Sebastian de Grazia, *The Political Community* (Chicago, 1948), pp. 129 ff.

4

1 Revised by R. C. Mortimer (London, 1947).

2 The Church of England Moral Welfare Council, Church House, 1961.

3 St. Augustine, *De Nupt. et Concup.* Lib. I, Ch. 17, and other places.

4 J. V. L. Casserley, op. cit., p. 188.

5 G. B. Bentley, in *Moral Problems* (London, 1954), p. 90.

6 R. C. Mortimer, Article 'Dearly Beloved' in

Getting Married, 1961 (British Medical Association).

7 On Christian Marriage, its nature and problems the following may be consulted: Anne Proctor, *Background to Marriage* (London, 1953); K. E. Kirk, *Marriage and Divorce* (London, 1948); Reginald Haw, *The State of Matrimony* (London, 1952); Gustave Thibon, *Ce que Dieu a Uni* (Paris, 1947). Eng. Tr., *Love and Marriage* (Universe Books, 1962); Erwin Reisner, *Vom Ursinn der Geschlechter*. French translation, *Métaphysique de la Sexualité* (Paris, Plon, 1960).

5

1 Anders Nygren, *Agape and Eros* (Eng. Tr., Philadelphia, 1953).

2 New York, 1955.

3 London, 1938.

4 *I and Thou* (Eng. Tr., 1937); *Between Man and Man* (Eng. Tr., 1947).

5 On previous life styles brought into marriage, see Alfred Adler, *Understanding Human Nature* (Eng. Tr., London, 1927); Erwin Wexberg, *Individual Psychology and Sex* (Eng. Tr., London, 1931).

6 Gustave Thibon, op. cit., pp. 64 ff.

7 Introduction to Miss Sayers' translation of Dante's *Divine Comedy*, II, *Purgatory* (Penguin Classics), p. 33.

6

1 Riddell Memorial Lectures (London, 1952).

2 *Vom Ursprung und Ziel der Geschichte* (Eng. Tr., *The Origin and Goal of History*, New Haven, 1953).
3 London, 1956.
4 New York, 1950.
5 Volume II, p. 351.
6 Eng. Tr., New York, 1953.
7 Cambridge, 1955.
8 London, 1953.
9 Eng. Tr., London, 1936.
10 Summarised in *Sexual Regulations and Cultural Behaviour* (Oxford, 1935).
11 New York, 1955.
12 Donald Macrae, *Britain's Long Decline, The Listener*, Nov. 23, 1961.

7

1 See J. Huizinga, op. cit.
2 New York, 1959, pp. 90, 91.
3 H.M. Stationery Office, 1960, pp. 32, 33.
4 T. M. Newcomb, *Recent Changes in Attitude to Sex and Marriage. American Sociological Review*, 1937. Polly Adler, *A House is not a Home* (New York, 1954).
5 De Grazia, op. cit., pp. 142, 144.
6 op. cit., p. 167.
7 op. cit., Chapter on *The Modern Family*.
8 *Male and Female*, pp. 353 ff.